HOLIDAY CRUISING IN IRELAND

Uniform with this book

HOLIDAY CRUISING ON INLAND WATERWAYS
by Charles Hadfield and Michael Streat

HOLIDAY CRUISING ON THE THAMES
by E. and P. W. Ball

A four-berth cruiser hired on the Shannon passes northwards through Monasterevin drawbridge, on the Barrow Line of the Grand Canal

HOLIDAY CRUISING IN IRELAND

A guide to Irish inland waterways

by

P. J. G. RANSOM

DAVID & CHARLES: NEWTON ABBOT

ISBN 0 7153 5003 X

The author has done his best to make sure that the information given in this book was correct when it went to press, but he cannot hold himself responsible for the consequences of any mistakes

Set in 11 pt Times New Roman 2 pt leaded
and printed in Great Britain
by Latimer Trend & Company Limited Plymouth
for David & Charles (Publishers) Limited
South Devon House Newton Abbot Devon

Contents

List of Illustrations

PLATES

All photographs not otherwise acknowledged are by the author

List of Illustrations

MAPS

Preface

It is, of course, an impertinence that a book which describes Irish waterways should be written by a visitor from England. But three-quarters of those who hire boats on the Shannon are British, I understand, so it is appropriate to write in terms which are most useful to them. (A more apt title might be *Irish Waterways for English Visitors.*) At any rate, during 1969 I cruised on all suitable Irish inland waterways, which is some excuse for writing about them, although one could spend a lifetime exploring any one of the big loughs alone, and I have been much helped by local experts.

These are some of the few Irish people who take an interest in inland waterways, for apart from the British, most other hirers are German, French or Swiss. I hope more Irish will take advantage of the improvements being made to the waterways, in the interest of tourism, by their governments with their money: otherwise the Shannon at least will become a river of foreigners.

In 1968 David & Charles published *Holiday Cruising on Inland Waterways*, a general introduction to the subject which beginners should tackle before this book, which complements it. I have avoided duplication of basic information, confining it to things which are peculiar to Ireland, or particularly important there, or at least unfamiliar to navigators of English waterways. In the gazetteer chapters I omit information (such as details of waterside archaeological remains) which is readily available in guidebooks; but in Chapter One I have included much general information for visitors—for English people tend to have fixed ideas about Ireland and the Irish, and many of them are wrong.

It has been suggested to me that true Irishmen will hate to have an Englishman come along and tell them *in detail* how bad their waterways are. And quite right too! Where I detail difficulties, it is not with intent to criticise, but rather to inform—to inform those about to cruise in Ireland what, on the basis of my own experience, they may expect to find, bad as well as good. This is what an independent cruising guide is for. So far as the condition of Irish waterways is concerned, taking all the circumstances into account there is little to criticise and much to praise.

The information given is according to the best available sources. Prices quoted are those current in 1970. However, it will be remarkable if no errors intrude, and in any event the rate of change on Irish waterways is such that the book will start to go out of date as soon as it is written. I cannot hold myself responsible for the consequences of any inaccuracies: E & OE. Nor does the mention of any waterway, mooring or quay imply any right to navigate, moor or land.

LATE NEWS

It is pleasing to record the following developments since the text was prepared:

Barrow: further dredging of lock cuts, repairs to locks and efforts to control weed growth (see page 81).

Shannon: dredging of mouth of Rinn River and establishment of hire base at Cloonart Bridge (see page 55); publication of a new edition of the *Shannon Guide* (see page 40).

CHAPTER ONE

Why Ireland?

The lock was going to be difficult. I was single-handed, there was a bridge rising sheer from the walls of the chamber, and nowhere below the lock to which I could tow the boat to rejoin her. The lock-keeper at the previous lock had declined to accompany me, remarking that I would have plenty of assistance. There was no one in sight. I was tired, cold, wet and hungry. The damp dripped off the trees and the rain was coming on again. And moored to one of the lock gates, blocking the entrance, was a small blue dinghy.

I knocked at the door of a nearby house, with some trepidation, to inquire if it might be possible to have the dinghy moved.

It was, of course. People young and old issued from the house. They moved the dinghy, helped me through the lock, opened and shut gates, hoisted and lowered racks. I was invited to moor alongside another boat, below the lock, and come indoors. I was sat in front of a blazing fire, so hot that people started to move away; I started to warm up and dry out. I must meet—, and—, and—, and—. There seemed to be about fifteen young people there. And would I like ham sandwiches? and cheese sandwiches? and cake? and coffee? and whiskey? I accepted them all, I am afraid, with more greed than good manners.

Such delightful extremes of Irish hospitality to strangers may not, I fear, survive any great inflation in the numbers of boats that pass. But if asked to name the pleasantest feature of an Irish cruising holiday I would suggest the certainty of a welcome at the end of the day's journey. Hospitality and friendliness towards strangers are a dominant Irish characteristic. First-time English visitors are sometimes overwhelmed to be greeted by total strangers with a warmth that they themselves reserve for close friends.

LOUGH, RIVER AND CANAL

There is little in England to resemble the Irish inland waterways. The large lakes or loughs ('lough' is pronounced like 'lock' or 'loch') of Ree, Derg, Corrib, Erne and Neagh are inland seas: from one end, the other is often indistinct and sometimes invisible. They are the terror of the novice and the delight of those with a little more experience—dangerous in foul weather and marvellous in fair, which is far more frequent. Flowing in and out of them are majestic rivers—notably the Shannon, which links Loughs Derg and Ree with many smaller lakes, and the Bann, which links Lough Neagh with the sea. Other smaller rivers are tributaries. Both lakes and rivers are often rocky and more hazardous than English rivers. They are also more rewarding. And then there is the Grand Canal, which links Dublin with the Rivers Shannon and Barrow: similar to, yet quite distinct from, the English canals.

Water is usually much clearer and cleaner than in English waterways—so much so that it is extracted from the Grand Canal to brew Guinness. Perhaps it was knowledge of this that led one of my party, who had the misfortune to find some tadpoles in his drink, to suppose they had arrived there through the brewing process; to the immense hilarity of his so-called friends, who had fished them from a puddle in the Bog of Allen and introduced them surreptitiously to his glass. Canal water for Guinness does pass through filter beds before reaching the brewery.

There are no tunnels on Irish waterways, no flights of locks with more than two connected chambers and no narrow locks, by English standards. There are also no longer any trading, cargo-carrying barges, except for some specialised traffic on Lough Neagh and the Bann. Pleasure craft share the waterways only with waterfowl, fish and fishermen. On the Shannon, the busiest pleasure cruising waterway, there are only about 350 privately owned craft and about 150 hire craft, with plans to increase the latter to around 300. So large is the Shannon that it is claimed that for it to reach the same density of boats as the Norfolk Broads would need 200,000 craft. The sense of space on water is matched on shore: the population of the whole of Ireland is less than 4½ million, or roughly half that of London. In the country, habitations are evenly spaced, so that Ireland, if under-populated, is never deserted. However, to me one of the delights of an Irish holiday is the sense of release from urban pressures.

TOPOGRAPHY AND TURF

The island of Ireland is customarily likened to a saucer, with a rim of mountains (chipped, presumably, where rivers escape to the sea) surrounding the central limestone plain. Much of the east resembles the English Midlands, without their industrial cities; the west is more shaggy. Rainfall is high, but the sun also shines and I have sweltered for a fortnight while London suffered a continuous drenching. July and August are the warmest months but May and June have more sunshine.

Heavy rainfall and poor drainage have turned much of the central plain into peat bog, formed by growth and decay of sphagnum moss and other plants. Bogland, seen to advantage from the Grand Canal, is an open wilderness of heath, marsh and copse which stretches away level to the horizon, its shades of green, brown and silver changing as sunlight succeeds shadow. Traditionally peat, or turf, is cut by hand, dried and used as fuel; recently Bord na Mona (the peat development authority), has developed mechanical turf harvesting. The turf is carried by light railway to turf-burning electric power stations and to factories which make it into briquettes for fuel. All this is seen from the waterways.

POLITICS AND THE PAST

Ireland is partitioned in two. Six counties, forming an area called Northern Ireland, are part of the United Kingdom, and have also a regional parliament in Belfast. Lough Neagh, the Lower Bann Navigation and most of the Erne are in Northern Ireland. The other twenty-six counties containing the rest of the waterways, though for many centuries linked administratively with the rest of the British Isles, are now the independent Republic of Ireland, with Dublin as its capital. While the republic claims the whole island, Northern Ireland seems happy to be known as Ulster, although it contains only six of the nine counties which formed that ancient province. And so the debate continues.

The reasons for partition result from history. Ireland, like other west European countries, was invaded many times. Most invaders or their descendants were eventually assimilated into the earlier Celtic population, who were always independent in spirit if not in fact. The most recent arrivals have not been assimilated. They came in the seventeenth century from Scotland and England to settle in the north-east. That they and their descendants remained distinct may in part be due to their Protestant religion, which separated them from those already there. In Ireland, even now, one's faith, Catholic or Protestant, is as much an indication of racial descent as religious conviction. About 95 per cent of the inhabitants of the republic are Catholic; in Northern Ireland, about two-thirds are Protestant, one-third Catholic.

There are those to whom the political status of Northern Ireland is unsatisfactory, and there has, over the past year or two, been Trouble. But not enough to hinder enjoyment of a cruising holiday. While cruising Loughs Erne and Neagh in September 1969 I would have been unaware anything was wrong had I not looked at the newspapers. Even the most ardent revolutionary would find throwing petrol bombs into the 53 sq miles of Lough Erne a frustrating business!

This description of Irish politics is an over-simplification, but further discussion, in a boating book, is out of place. Another happier point of Irish history is relevant: early Christian saints, who established monasteries in Ireland from the sixth century onwards, found suitable sites close to the water. Ecclesiastical remains, and the round towers beside them, built as refuges in time of war, fascinate visitors by boat.

PEOPLE AND THINGS

Irish countryside is everywhere unspoilt and pleasant, and well known for its greenness. But in the republic, other colours are always subdued—for instance, bridges along the Grand Canal, though handsome, are built from cool grey limestone —one misses the warm red brick of the English canals—and buildings are usually stone, or rough-cast, or concrete; or if painted, are in pastel colours. So that a lot of the attraction of Ireland depends on its people.

The Irishman in England, wheeling his barrow on a building site, is a poor advertisement for his fellow countrymen. However, he is, after all, fed up and far from home in a strange and seemingly rather hostile land. Irish people in Ireland, in addition to being hospitable and friendly, are helpful, well informed, eloquent, argumentative (for its own sake) unpretentious, imaginative, full of great ideas but lacking in concern for detail, stubborn, proud (without being vain)— in a word, inconsistent—and often lacking in perception of visual beauty but possessing in compensation a flair for things rhythmical and musical. They also have an overriding sense of fun and gaiety. The latter characteristics are experienced at their best in an evening of songs and ballads in a waterside pub. (The tonnage of ale and stout carried on Irish railways is only very slightly less than the tonnage of oil.)

The Irish language, a Celtic tongue of—in writing—awe-inspiring, jaw-breaking, appearance, has been revived; but knowledge of it is unnecessary for visitors, except perhaps to bear in mind that a 'garda' is a policeman (in full, 'garda siochana', a guardian of the peace) and that 'fir' are gents and 'mna' (which looks like 'men') are ladies. There are quite a few Irishisms in English, as spoken, which enliven holiday conversations.

It is not only people, though. At every quay and lock, on the busy waterways, there seems to be a large and friendly dog, who knows very well that boats come along to feed him!

In Ireland, old and new exist side by side. For example, there used to be an Irish mile, of 2,240yd, and there are mile-stones along the Grand Canal marked in Irish miles to this day. The Shannon Navigation plans to indicate distances in kilometres. And the cream that accompanies your coffee in an Aer Lingus (Irish Airlines) Boeing is aseptically processed, packed in a triangular sided carton. It probably went to the creamery in a churn on a donkey cart. The hours of the clock are the same as in Britain; Ireland being farther west, this means it gets dark later. I noted, one fine June evening, a glow in the sky until after midnight. By 9 am the following day the sun was hot and high from the opposite direction. So far as timekeeping is concerned, things tend to happen rather slowly.

Shops in the republic are often open much later than in England, and early closing days are staggered. Usual banking hours are 10.0 am to 12.30 pm and 1.30 pm to 3.0 pm, but some small branches are open only for limited hours and days. Pubs are open on weekdays from 10.30 am to 11.30 pm, with in some places an hour's closing during the after-noon, and in winter 'early closing' at 11.00 pm; and on Sundays from 12.30 pm to 2.0 pm and 4.0 pm to 10.00 pm. Bank holidays, during the cruising season, are 17 March (St Patrick's Day), Good Friday, Easter Monday, and the first Mondays in June and August. Telephoning is a leisurely pursuit; in the country, telephones often still work on the turn handle—lift receiver—and wait for the operator principle and it takes perhaps half an hour to get a call through to England. The coin boxes do not accept English sixpences. Medical attention, for visitors who need it, must be paid for.

Northern Irish people are more like Scottish or English, although as hospitable as Irish, without perhaps the same instant friendliness. They are usually more efficient (at times almost to the point of officiousness). Northern Ireland shop hours are similar to England, banks are open from 10.0 am to 3.30 pm, but closed for one hour for lunch and open longer hours on Fridays. Pubs are open from 10 am to 10 pm on weekdays but closed on Sundays. Bank holidays are 17 March, Good Friday, Easter Monday, Whit Monday, 12 July and the first Monday in September. The National Health Service functions, and so does subscriber trunk dialling, though no better than in England.

The monetary unit in the Irish Republic is the Irish pound, maintained at parity with the pound sterling. There are Irish bank notes (issued by the Central Bank of Ireland) and Irish coins. But both these and British coins and Bank of England notes circulate freely throughout both the republic and Northern Ireland. In addition, some banks in Northern Ireland issue their own notes, comparable to those issued by Scottish banks. Many Irish banks cash cheques on presentation of a cheque card or Barclaycard. The republic plans to introduce decimal currency on 15 February 1971, the same date as the UK.

FISHING

Ireland is famous for its fishing, which is well publicised

Whether cruising and fishing holidays can be successfully combined is, I think, doubtful, and depends on the participants; in any event, anglers have their own sources of information, and must excuse me from describing fishing here. Those wanting advice could try, for a start, the tourist boards.

WATERWAY BACKGROUND

The waterway history of Ireland is fascinating and well described in *The Canals of the South of Ireland* by V. T. H. & D. R. Delany, and *The Canals of the North of Ireland* by W. A. McCutcheon, both published by David & Charles; and two booklets, *Coastal Passenger Steamers and Inland Navigations in the North of Ireland* and *Coastal Passenger Steamers and Inland Navigations in the South of Ireland*, both by D. B. McNeill and published by Belfast Transport Museum. The eighteenth century and the early part of the nineteenth saw a boom in building canals, and making river navigations by constructing weirs to maintain the depth of water and locks for boats to pass the weirs; followed by much passenger and freight traffic, worked by horse-drawn and sailing vessels and pioneer steamers. Railways later took most of the passenger traffic but a lot of freight remained on the water until the rise of motor road transport in this century. Many canals have since been closed.

Concurrent with the decline in waterway trade (which, after all, still flourishes on the Continent and elsewhere) grew concern for the survival of waterways and an increase in pleasure cruising. The Inland Waterways Association of Ireland was founded in 1954 to promote the use, development and maintenance of navigable waterways. Its early successes were to prevent construction of a low bridge without headroom for boats at Athlone, midway along the Shannon, which would have strangled the waterway; and opposition to a clause in the Transport Act, 1958, which would have permitted closure of the Grand Canal. There have been many other achievements. Recently the fight has been over the Grand Canal through Dublin—although it is one of the city's pleasantest amenities, the authorities coveted its route for use as a sewer and/or a road. Happily the latest proposal for the sewer does not involve closing the canal.

In Northern Ireland, the proposal in 1962 to abandon the Lower Bann Navigation prompted formation of the River Bann Association, with similar objects, in its area, to the IWAI.

Pleasure cruising in Ireland is very old established—the Lough Erne Yacht Club was founded as early as 1820; but it is the recent increase that is remarkable. The number of craft passing through Albert Lock on the Shannon rose from 70 in 1959 to 2,240 in 1969. The increase in the popularity of cruising and the growth of hire fleets owe a lot to publicity and financial grants by Bord Failte Eireann (the Irish Tourist Board; 'Failte' pronounced 'Forlsher'). Hire operators get grants of 40 per cent of the cost of new craft, and up to 1969 £232,800 had been spent on or allocated for improvements to the Shannon Navigation, carried out in conjunction with the navigation authority (the Board of Works) and county councils. The Northern Ireland Tourist Board likewise promotes cruising on the Erne.

Along with the growth of cruising have developed boat rallies—notably on the Shannon and Erne, organised by local branches of the IWAI, and on the Bann, organised by the River Bann Association. Waterside festivals are held in summer beside the Grand Canal at Robertstown and Dublin.

FLOATELS AND EXCURSIONS

There are three ways to explore Irish waterways: to go on a public cruise, by hotel boat or day excursion; to hire a cruiser and run it yourself; or to use your own boat. The latter two choices produce an adventurous holiday—a hire cruiser needs at least two people who are active and capable of handling it; and no matter how much money is spent on improvements to the waterways it can neither moderate the gales nor soften the rocks. So the first possibility is worth careful consideration. It includes a guide familiar with the waterway and freedom from worries of navigation and catering.

Irish River Floatels Ltd, Athlone, County Westmeath, operate all-services-provided hotel craft on which 'relaxation is the keynote'. They cover the Shannon from Athlone to Killaloe or Carrick in alternate weeks, from Thursday to Thursday. Included in the charge of 34 gn (£35.70) for a week's cruise and 59 gn (£61.95) for a fortnight are transport between Dublin and Athlone and coach tours to Limerick (lower Shannon cruise) and to Sligo and to Galway (upper Shannon cruise). Weaver Boats Ltd, 9 Duke Lane, Dublin, run Saturday-to-Saturday cruises by well converted barges on the Shannon from Lanesborough to Lough Key and back. Participants swim, sail, fish, sketch, take photographs, play musical instruments, sit in the sun and help to operate the boats. All-in cost for a week in the high season is £22 a person, and the formula is successful enough for a third barge to be added in 1970 to the two already in use.

Day cruises are operated by motor vessel by Coras Iompair Eireann (CIE, the Irish transport system) on Lough Derg, from Killaloe, and Lough Ree, from Athlone. On Lough Corrib, Dolan Bros run a modern waterbus daily from Woodquay, Galway; and on Lough Neagh, a large modern vessel, the *Maid of Antrim*, owned by H. McGarry & Sons, Ardmore Boat Yard, Crumlin, Co Antrim, runs daily cruises from the mouth of the Six Mile Water, near Antrim town. A craft called *Endeavour* runs cruises on the Erne from Round O Quay, Enniskillen. All these cruises run only in summer.

CRUISE PLANNING—HIRED AND PRIVATELY OWNED CRAFT

Boats for Irish inland waterways need to be more seaworthy

than for English rivers and canals, and should be fairly low in the water to reduce the effect of side winds. Distances travelled depend so much on the inclination of the crew, the type of waterway, the weather, the number of locks and the speed of the boat that it is impossible to give useful general guidance, except to mention that the relatively heavily locked Grand Canal system is slow, and to go down the Shannon from Carrick to Killaloe and back needs a fortnight's holiday.

For beginners to cruising the most suitable water in Ireland is in my opinion Upper Lough Erne (qv) followed by the Shannon above Tarmonbarry.

When planning a cruise which covers any of the big loughs, it is essential to include a day or two of 'slack' in the programme to allow for being caught in harbour by bad weather; and when planning an extensive cruise, it is worth inquiring of the navigation authorities whether any stoppages are planned. With the absence of commercial traffic, repairs to locks, etc, are not always made with great alacrity.

HIRE CRAFT

Hire craft are available on the Shannon Navigation, the Grand Canal, the River Barrow Navigation and the Erne.

There are three associations of hire operators: the Charter Boat Association of Ireland (the Swan Fleet), with members indicated 'C' below; Irish Hire Boat Operators Ltd (the Penguin Group), with members indicated 'P' below; and the Erne Charter Boat Association, with members indicated 'E' below (all the Erne hire operators). Addresses of these associations are given at the end of the book.

Combined brochures are issued by the Penguin Group and the Erne association, the latter under the name *Cruise the Lovely Erne Waterway*: other hire operators issue their own literature. Waterway maps included in these, which prospective hirers might reasonably be expected to assume show waterways navigable by the boats offered, sometimes include inaccuracies. For example, three 1970 brochures have maps which include Lough Allen, although that lake is inaccessible from the Shannon. Weekly hire rates range from £16 16s (£16.80) for a two-berth cruiser out of season to £111 for an eight-berth cruiser in the high season. Embarkation day is usually Saturday but Erne hire operators offer Thursday-to-Thursday bookings and Joy Line Wednesday-to-Wednesday.

The principal hire operators offering motor cruisers in 1970 were the following:

Waterway and base	Hire operator	Address for inquiries and bookings (Irish Republic except where otherwise shown)	Boats accommodate this number of people: Min	Max	Association (see above)
Shannon					
Cootehall	Shannon Cruisers Ltd	Cootehall, Boyle, Co Roscommon	2	6	P
Carrick	Mitchell Marine Ltd	Carrick on Shannon, Co Leitrim	2	6	P
,,	Emerald Star Line Ltd. ('A company within the Guinness Group')	St James's Gate, Dublin	4	8	P
,,	Carrick Craft	Waveney Hotel & Yacht Station, Burgh St Peter, Nr Beccles, Norfolk, England	4	6	
,,	Flag Line Ltd	Rosebank Marina, Carrick on Shannon, Co Leitrim	4	8	P
Jamestown	K Line Cruisers. (O'B Kennedy Sons & Co Ltd)	Jamestown, Drumsna, Co Leitrim	5	7	
Rooskey	Breffni Cruisers (Shannon) Ltd	Rooskey, Co Roscommon	3	9	
Cloonart Bridge	Holland Supercraft Ltd	36 Strathfield Gardens, Barking, Essex, England	5	5	
Athlone	Athlone Cruisers Ltd	Shancurragh, Athlone	3	8	C
,,	Shamrock Cruisers	'Cremona', Sli-an-Aifrinn, Athlone	4	4	
Banagher	Silver Line Cruisers	Banagher, Co Offaly	4	6	C
Killaloe	Cruising Craft (Shannon) Ltd	Lakeside Marina, Killaloe, Co Clare	2	6	P
,,	Cormacruises Ltd	,,	3	6	

Waterway and base	Hire operator	Address for inquiries and bookings (Irish Republic except where otherwise shown)	Boats accommodate this number of people: Min	Max	Association (see above)
Grand Canal					
Lowtown	Joy Line Cruisers Ltd	18 Berkeley St, Dublin 7	2	6	C
Twelfth Lock, Lucan	Leisure Line Cruisers Ltd	20 Temple Bar, Dublin 2	3	7	C
River Barrow Navigation					
Carlow	Barrow Line Holiday Cruisers Ltd	Dublin Road, Carlow	2	5	
Erne					
Belturbet	Book-a-Boat Ltd	Belturbet, Co Cavan. (1 Oct to 1 May: Drumully, Emyvale, Co Monaghan)	4	5	E
Carrybridge	Carrybridge Boat Co	1 The Limes, Lisbellaw, Co Fermanagh, Northern Ireland	2	4	E
Bellanaleck	Erne Hire Cruisers Ltd	32 East Bridge St, Enniskillen, Co Fermanagh, Northern Ireland	4	5	E
Bellanaleck	Erne Marine	Bellanaleck, Enniskillen, Co Fermanagh, Northern Ireland	5	7	E
near Kesh	Lakeland Marina Ltd	Kesh, Co Fermanagh, Northern Ireland	2	5	E

Many hire cruisers on Irish waterways are English built, and are of the same classes as hire cruisers on Norfolk Broads, Thames and Fens. Accommodation is comparable and boats with running hot water, showers and refrigerators are now available. About the only luxury that does not seem to be offered is television. Because hire cruising in Ireland is expanding rapidly, many of the cruisers are modern. The other side of this particular coin is that in Ireland as elsewhere it is as well to be wary of the boat that is described in the brochure as 'to be built for this season' and illustrated by drawing rather than photograph. Boat builders do not always deliver on time, and even if they do, boats have teething troubles and *you* do not wish to be the hirer immobilised by them. Hire operators on the Broads seem more pessimistic than those in Ireland about the number of people to be accommodated on a boat. For instance, boats of the same class are offered for two people on the Broads but four in Ireland.

Hire cruisers are well equipped, but there are some items which are worth inquiring about, to check if they are supplied, and whether or not at extra cost. These are: compass, binoculars (both essential for lake cruising); Admiralty charts (see below) for any large lakes to be visited, preferably with navigation markers added; radio (for weather forecast); barometer and echo sounder, although opinions vary on the usefulness of the latter; mooring stakes and hammer; spare fuel can and funnel to transfer its contents to the boat's fuel tank; garbage bin; heating for end-of-season cruises (at least one operator equips boats with turf-burning stoves, and what could be more appropriate?); and if you intend to visit the Grand Canal system, a lock key (windlass to English canallers) and plenty of fenders—at least eight. At the same time it is worth checking whether you can get at the propeller without entering the water, for on the canal you will certainly need access to remove weed etc.

Dinghys are supplied with hire cruisers on Shannon and Erne. In my experience those on the Shannon vary from the uncomfortable to the dangerous. The most recent example deposited its owner in the water shortly before my arrival—he greeted us with dripping trousers and a broad grin! No doubt there are many excellent and seaworthy dinghys on the Shannon and I have just been unlucky. Some hire operators supply sailing dinghys on request.

CRUISING BY SAIL

Sailing yachts with auxiliary engines, either inboard or outboard, are offered for hire on the Shannon by K Line Cruisers and Athlone Cruisers Ltd and on the Erne by Lakeland Marina Ltd. There are a few privately owned vessels. I am no sailing man, but it surprises me there are not more. A contributor to *Yachting & Boating Weekly* (26 February 1969) found Lough Derg 'absolutely intoxicating'. He was describing a cruise in search of quiet sailing waters from Glasson Dock, Lancaster to Killaloe and back, by way of the Irish Sea and Grand Canal. Lough Neagh could be visited similarly via the Lower Bann Navigation. There are yacht, sailing or boat clubs on all the large Irish lakes.

APPROACHES TO IRELAND

Visitors taking their own boat to Ireland either cruise there by sea or take it on a trailer by car ferry. Loughs Corrib and Erne are inaccessible from the sea, though they have launching ramps, but the Shannon/Grand Canal network can be approached from the sea via Dublin (Grand Canal), St Mullins (River Barrow Navigation) and Limerick (Shannon), and the Bann can be entered from the sea via Coleraine. Tidal approaches to Irish inland waterways are complicated; experts have their guides in the *Irish Coast Pilot* and two volumes published by the Irish Cruising Club: *Sailing Directions—East and North Coasts of Ireland* and *Sailing Directions—South and West Coasts of Ireland*, although they would find local advice also useful. In the gazetteer chapters which follow I have taken the line that inland waterways end where the tide begins. At the other end of the scale there are several lakes on which a fair sized boat could be placed, but they, and the Newry Ship Canal, are not extensive enough for a cruising holiday and so are omitted.

There are at the time of writing nine drive-on, drive-off, car ferry routes between Britain and Ireland with another promised; the principal operators are British Rail and B & I Line. Motoring organisations such as the Automobile Association have full information and *Which?* magazine published a comprehensive survey in January 1970. There is also a direct route from the Continent: Le Havre–Rosslare. Many sea routes also take passengers without cars, and there are others for passengers only; both have connecting trains.

The principal airports in Ireland of use to visitors to inland waterways are Dublin and Belfast, both an hour or so of flying time from London and many other British airports by British European Airways, Aer Lingus and other airlines. Shannon airport is near the estuary of the river and too far to the south-west to be convenient except for those starting their cruise at Killaloe.

All routes between Britain and Ireland are heavily booked far ahead for the main holiday season.

ACROSS THE BORDER

There are no restrictions on travel between Britain and Northern Ireland.

To cross between the UK and the Irish Republic, whether by air, sea, or land border, passports are not needed, but there are Customs regulations. The following notices, issued by the Revenue Commissioners, Dublin Castle, should be consulted as appropriate by intending visitors to the republic:

- No 533 Customs Guide for Visitors.
- No 18A Customs Guide for Visiting Motorists.
- No 18B Customs Guide for Visiting Caravanners (which includes visitors with boat-trailers).
- No 93 Notice to Owners and Masters of Yachts and other persons concerned—which details requirements for yachts on arrival from abroad by sea and on departure for foreign parts.

Cars, boat trailers and trailer-borne boats with ancillary equipment may be imported temporarily into the republic without payment of duty. The AA (which functions equally in the republic as in the UK) and similar organisations have details of further requirements.

The navigable Erne extends both sides of the border: Customs information is given in the chapter on that waterway.

GETTING TO THE WATER

Roads and motoring in Northern Ireland are similar to Britain. In the republic, roads are not as good, but they are less crowded and so better in relation to the amount of traffic. The equivalents of A and B roads are T(runk) and L(ink) roads. There is an overall 60mph speed limit and the Department of Local Government, O'Connell Bridge House, Dublin 2 issues a leaflet *Ireland—Traffic Rules* in English, French and German. The AA members' handbook for Ireland is a mine of information about both Northern Ireland and the republic.

Public transport in the Irish Republic, both rail and bus, is operated by CIE. Routes are extensive, services adequate though infrequent. Railway stations, at points on inland waterways outside Dublin, are Carrick on Shannon, Dromod and Athlone, on the Shannon; Tullamore, Athy, Carlow and Muine Bheag (Bagenalstown) on the Grand Canal and River Barrow Navigation; and Galway, on Lough Corrib. Other places are served by bus, either local or long distance.

Northern Ireland is served by Northern Ireland Railways and Ulsterbus, with greater frequencies than public transport in the republic. But the only places served by rail in the North of much use to inland navigators are Portadown and Antrim, close to Lough Neagh. Other places are served by bus. Enniskillen, on the Erne, has express buses from both Belfast (Ulsterbus) and Dublin (CIE).

Many hire operators on the Shannon now provide transport from Dublin for hirers. This is certainly a convenience but I have a suspicion that it is making things too easy. Anyone incapable of finding his own way to Carrick is unlikely to be self-reliant enough to navigate the Shannon successfully!

NEEDS AND SUPPLIES

Hot weather clothes are needed for summer cruises, plenty of warm clothes for end of season cruises and all-over waterproof clothes for any time of year. Yachting- or gum-boots are useful, for foliage grows abundantly around some quays and locks, gets wet from rain and quickly soaks shoes and trousers. Polaroid spectacles are valuable, not only to reduce glare, but also to help helmsmen to spot underwater obstructions. Insect repellent is worth having, and so is a good torch. Take a good general guide book, and add guides to wild flowers and birds, according to taste. Do not forget towels and matches.

Hire operators provide hirers with a grocery list and arrange for supplies ordered to be put on board. In Northern Ireland provisions come in much the same range and at similar prices to Britain. In the republic food is often more expensive, with the exception of fresh meat and bacon, which are cheap, locally produced and usually excellent. Cheese and salad materials are rare and green vegetables sometimes difficult to obtain. Irish-prepared tinned food is usually of better quality than British and tins of Irish stew are a useful standby. For drinkers, Guinness, of course, is everywhere, and so is Harp lager. Phoenix and Smithwicks beers resemble light ales and Power's Whiskey is always acceptable. These are personal preferences; there are other well-known brands. There is little difficulty in obtaining supplies: Irish village shops, often combined with pubs, are famous for selling everything (except meat, available only in towns and large villages). In the gazetteer chapters towns should have most services; at smaller places, I have indicated the services available.

Throughout Ireland, petrol prices are similar to Britain. Diesel fuel costs about 2s (10p) a gallon, if you can negotiate a supply free of the tax for road vehicle use. Hire operators supply it thus. Waterside refuelling points are few and far between.

ON THE MOVE, AT LAST

The basic principles of handling a boat, set out in Chapter Four of *Holiday Cruising on Inland Waterways*, apply as much in Ireland as elsewhere, and so does the rule of the road—keep to the right (pass port to port).

On four Irish waterways—Shannon, Corrib, Erne and Lower Bann—the navigation channel, and obstructions to it, are indicated by markers. These are either buoys, beacons (which are conical mounds of stone) or perches (which are posts). Markers are painted in distinctive colours and/or carry 'topmarks' of distinctive shape, according to which side boats must pass them. Details of the system in use on each waterway are described in the appropriate chapter.

It is essential to keep a sharp look out for markers and to pass them on the correct side—on the wrong side are shallow water and, perhaps, rocks. Boats should not moor to markers: this hides them and puts other boats in danger. On winding courses, markers sometimes appear, in the distance, the 'wrong way round', that is, a port marker to the right of a starboard one; the course zigzags between them.

At bridges with many arches usually only one, or occasionally two, are free from underwater obstructions to boats. Identification of these 'navigation arches' varies from waterway to waterway and is described in the appropriate chapters. Some bridges have opening spans. These may or may not need to be opened, according to the headroom required by individual boats, but the navigation channel invariably passes beneath them.

There are innumerable maps and charts of Irish waterways,

and none of them is perfect. The Admiralty, in the mid-nineteenth century, had surveys made of Loughs Ree, Derg, Corrib, Erne (Upper and Lower) and Neagh. Although water levels have since altered, as detailed in the relevant chapters, the Admiralty charts are still essential for anyone navigating these loughs. They are obtainable from Admiralty chart agents. Since English inland waterway people are unfamiliar with Admiralty charts, it is worth mentioning that they are, generally, self-explanatory; they are in black and white, without distinctive colours for land and water; but water areas are immediately distinguishable because they are covered in figures: these are soundings, recording the depth of water in feet.

Unfortunately the Admiralty charts are out of date regarding positions of quays and too old to show navigation markers. I have tried to remedy this deficiency to some extent in the lake maps included in this book. These show courses in relation to shore, islands, quays and, where possible, markers. They are to be used with the appropriate Admiralty charts, where available. The lake maps are all to the same scale and north is always at the top[1]. However, navigation markers are often added, damaged or replaced and any map which shows them rapidly goes out of date. Rivers, therefore, and canals are shown here in stylised strip map form, which enables complicated sections to be shown clearly. On the Shannon, a chain of lakes connected by river, lake maps and strip maps alternate. A few lakes are shown stylised on the strip maps.

In Northern Ireland, one inch to the mile Ordnance Survey maps are produced, similar to those in England, and kept up to date. The Ordnance Survey office of the Irish Republic concentrates on half-inch to the mile maps, which are up to date and readily available: most one-inch scale maps have not been revised for over fifty years and are available in black and white from the Ordnance Survey Office, Phoenix Park, Dublin. Regrettably none of these maps shows the position of all locks and weirs.

[1] A note about symbols on maps appears on page 130.

CRUISING THE LOUGHS

To cruise the big loughs, clear weather and a good pair of binoculars are essential (for spotting distant navigation markers, which may be a couple of miles apart), and so is a compass. Besides confirming that the course is correct, the compass indicates the direction in which the next marker or harbour will appear. It is essential to know where you are at all times on the loughs, and if mist or rain looks like obscuring the next marker, to take a compass bearing on it and steer by that. In a cross wind it is necessary to look astern from time to time to ensure that your course is straight from marker to marker and that you are not being blown off course into shallow water. At promontories, beacons close to the shore which sufficed for professional boatmen have sometimes been supplemented by perches or buoys further out which mark the actual limit of shallow water. When a conspicuous marker is in view in the distance, it is necessary to check to see that there are no nearer, less conspicuous, markers to indicate a deviation from the direct course.

Before setting out, knowledge of the weather forecast and state of the barometer is desirable. Conditions in sheltered harbours are sometimes deceptively calm. All the large Irish loughs have ugly reputations for rough seas and changeability. Locals ascribe the cause variously to the presence of mountains (Derg, Corrib, Erne) which 'affect the air currents' or the absence of mountains (Ree, Neagh)—'no shelter'! Anyway, waves are shorter and steeper than those met at sea in similar wind conditions. Apart from danger to boats themselves they make navigation markers such as buoys difficult to see in the distance. The danger point comes when the wind reaches force five (according to the Beaufort scale: 'small trees in leaf begin to sway, crested wavelets on inland waters, moderate waves and many white horses at sea'—Irish loughs seem to come somewhere between the two). When the wind reaches force six it is time to be tucked away in a nice cosy harbour. Experienced sailors, of course, will use their own judgement. If the weather deteriorates rapidly after you have gone out on to one of the loughs, there is no shame in turning back. The wind often moderates towards evening and does not get up for a while in the morning.

The shores of lakes and rivers are usually shallow and rocky or reedy; off points and islands the bottom shelves particularly gently. It is dangerous to hug the bank when cruising, and it is unusual to be able to moor to it except on the canal. Generally it is necessary to go from quay to quay—to go ashore elsewhere, the cruiser should be anchored and the dinghy used.

For an anchor to function, it must lie on the bottom. This means it needs a length of chain between anchor and rope, to weigh it down, and the length of rope paid out must be at least three times the depth of water. To go astern briefly after anchoring helps to dig the anchor in and checks that it is holding—for the bottom of many Irish inland waterways is notoriously bad holding ground for anchors. Because of this, and the danger of sudden deterioration in the weather, hire operators recommend that hirers should not anchor overnight but should moor at quays.

Should you be unfortunate enough to be blown on to a lee shore, it is better not to risk propeller damage by trying to get off under power, but to take the anchor up wind by dinghy to the full extent of its rope, drop it and haul or 'kedge' the cruiser off against it.

Coming alongside a quay is easiest against wind and current or whichever is stronger. If this is impossible, for instance at the approach to a lock, whoever goes ashore should take the stern rope: to take the bow rope ashore simply means that the stern will swing out.

Page 33 Shannon Navigation: (*above*) Athlone, looking upstream from the east bank quay. The navigation span of the bridge is next the far bank; (*below*) the expanse of Lough Derg reduces CIE's 200 passenger mv *St Ciaran* to a speck. This is only a small part of the lake, looking from the east shore towards (left to right) Aughinish Point, Lushing Rocks (which look like an island) and Scilly Island, with Scariff Bay beyond

Page 34 (*above*) Shannon Navigation: October sunshine briefly illuminates Rockingham Harbour, Lough Key, and Castle Island. Following the navigation course, the hire cruiser shown has approached from the left distance; (*below*) Grand Canal, Shannon Line. Looking east at Chevenix Bridge, at the start of the long level above the six locks by which the canal climbs out of Tullamore

INCIDENTS AND ACCIDENTS

It is a remarkable hire craft that never breaks down. Hire operators, with a natural reluctance to encourage unskilled hirers to tinker, usually supply only a minimum of tools. However, some have no objection to minor defects, such as flat batteries, being cured locally. For more serious defects the hire operator should be contacted by telephone. It is as well to establish, before taking over a boat, what procedure the owner wishes followed; and for English visitors to remember that telephoning and waiting for assistance to come require patience.

In the event of a breakdown off-shore, the first thing to do is anchor, to prevent the boat drifting into shallow water. If you are unable to remedy the trouble yourself (fuel tank empty?) you are almost certainly safer on the cruiser waiting for help to arrive than going for help in the dinghy, particularly if it is at all rough. On the navigation course on Shannon or Erne it is unlikely to be long before another boat passes.

Hire craft are equipped with distress smoke flares to attract attention, but they should only be used in the event of a real emergency, for other people and boats may endanger themselves coming to the rescue.

If you go aground, you must be in shallow water and in no great danger. Athlone Cruisers Ltd, one of the most experienced Shannon hire firms, give the following instruction to hirers in this situation:

1. Put on life-jackets.
2. If still on the rock or shoal, do not move the cruiser until sure she is not holed. Even if badly holed, you will still be safe on the rock.
3. Lift floorboards and check for leaks. There may already have been water in the bilge—pump or bucket it out and see if the level rises. If you find a hole, stuff blankets into it.

4. If satisfied there is no hole, try to get the boat off the shoal, either by reversing the engine, or by getting everyone to move to the free end or side, or by kedging it off.

5. If this fails, wait for a passing boat. Think twice before going for assistance in the dinghy.

6. If you strike a rock and bounce off, becoming holed in the process, put on life-jackets, bail and pump, and head for shallow water, if need be back on to the shoal. If you can stuff blankets into the hole do so, but do not waste time looking for a hole while the boat is sinking. Stay with the boat as long as possible; she will not suddenly sink like a stone and if you run her aground you will be safe. Only abandon ship as a last resort.

Should you see another boat which appears to be aground, it is not recommended to rush straight in to its assistance, unless you wish to join it on the rocks! Use the dinghy, if possible.

Hire craft are equipped with buoyancy jackets for all the crew, so there is no excuse for not wearing them. The most likely times for someone to go overboard are during the bustle of leaving and approaching quays and passing through locks. People in the water are difficult to spot. When someone goes overboard, whoever sees them go should watch them until they are picked up. A lifebelt should be thrown as close as possible without actually hitting them, and the boat turned so as to head into the wind while they are being picked up.

All of which may suggest that cruising in Ireland, when not actually dangerous, is rather dull. It is not. It is tremendous fun.

CHAPTER TWO

The Shannon Navigation[1]

The Shannon is vast—too vast to sum up briefly. Not that the vastness of the waterway is obvious (although it is immediately apparent that its width is much greater than, say, the Oxford Canal). The river twists and turns, and even on lakes where there are views of 10 miles or more there is no sign that these are equalled elsewhere on a navigation of some 145 route miles, which includes two large lakes and eleven small ones.

The position of the Shannon in Ireland is comparable to that of the Severn in England, and it is best described in five sections. From its northern navigable limit at Battlebridge via Carrick on Shannon to Lanesborough the river winds between low hills and expands into frequent small lakes which are as long as 2 or 3 miles. The hills are mostly drumlins, relics of glacial action; straggling hedges of thorn separate rough fields and thatched and whitewashed single-storey cottages are accompanied by small round haystacks. Many tributaries are navigable and the whole area is the most popular in Ireland for hire cruising. Below Lanesborough is Lough Ree, some 18 miles long and from 1 to 7 miles wide, 39 sq miles of island speckled water.

From Athlone, at the south end of Lough Ree, to Portumna the river meanders through remote flat country, deploys backwaters which disappear round extensive islands, and floods excessively in winter. Below Portumna the river enters

[1] See pages 131 to 133 for Shannon Navigation strip maps.

Lough Derg—24 miles long and 2 or 3 miles wide, with many deeper indentations along its shores. Here the waterway leaves the plain, and the approaches to Killaloe, at the south end of the lake, are flanked by hills more than 1,500ft high. Killaloe (pronounced Killaloo) is the limit set by many hire operators; beyond it an ill-marked channel follows artificial waterways to the lock and hydro-electric generating station at Ardnacrusha. Below Ardnacrusha the river is tidal.

Work on making the Shannon navigable commenced in 1755, but it is improvements carried out in the early 1840s that today form the basis of the navigation above Killaloe, though remains of earlier works can be seen. The navigation authority is the Office of Public Works (colloquially, the Board of Works), 51 St Stephen's Green, Dublin 2. The Electricity Supply Board has statutory powers over the Shannon in connection with Ardnacrusha power station. These include the right (now seldom used) to prohibit navigation for limited periods of time, and the right to alter the levels of the lakes. In practice, Lough Derg is maintained at a fairly constant level, but Lough Ree fluctuates.

Boats do not need to be licensed, nor are there mooring charges at public quays, but new bye-laws are being prepared to include registration of boats and owners. A lock fee of 3s 4½d (nearest decimal equivalent 17p) is payable to lock-keepers for passing through each lock. There are five locks on the main line of navigation between Battlebridge and Killaloe; one on the Boyle River, a tributary; two on a branch into Richmond Harbour; one at Killaloe which it is normally possible to avoid; and a deep double lock at the power station at Ardnacrusha. Access from the sea is limited to boats which need maximum headroom of 9ft 6in[1] and can get through the 19ft 6in wide by 105ft long chambers of the lock at Ardnacrusha; above Killaloe, all the main line locks, and that on the Boyle River, are at least 30ft wide by 102ft long. Locks

[1] This is the clearance at Ardnacrusha Lock. Limerick bridges may impose lower headroom.

are operated by lock-keepers at all reasonable hours between sunrise and sunset, although hours may be more limited in future. Each lock cottage now has a telephone available for use by passing boaters. The maximum draught of boats able to cruise the whole navigation is 4ft 6in, and the minimum head-room of fixed bridges is 16ft 6in above Killaloe and 13ft below.

Navigation markers are buoys, beacons or perches; those to be left to port when going upstream or entering bays and harbours are painted red, and those to be left to starboard when going upstream or entering bays and harbours are painted black. Some, but not all, have disc topmarks: red topmarks are round and black topmarks are square or rectangular. Both often have holes to reduce wind resistance. Buoys of several sizes are used, from small barrels to large estuary type buoys in the lakes; their colours are often defaced by cormorants which perch on them. Against a low sun it is sometimes impossible to distinguish the colour of small buoys without topmarks until within a few feet: extreme care is then needed, as buoys sometimes appear in unexpected positions. There is no identification on markers, but it is proposed to mark some of the large buoys with their distance in km from Ardnacrusha. Shoals in the lakes are usually rock, those in river sections usually gravel or boulder clay but sometimes rock. Reed beds line much of the shore: pale bamboo-like reeds with leaves and feathery tops indicate shallow water, but dark green reeds like big rushes without leaves but with small feathery tops grow in depths down to about 5ft and may be approached cautiously. Shores free of reeds are usually either too rocky or too exposed to support them.

Navigation arches of bridges have a patch of red or black paint each side, to be treated in the same way as navigation markers. Some bridges have opening or lifting spans but most cruisers can pass below them when closed except for those at Portumna and, in some instances, Tarmonbarry. The fee for having a bridge opened is the same as the lock fee. Electric cables cross the navigation at many places; the usual clearance, above Killaloe, is 35ft above normal summer level. All islands are private property, but visits to those with archaeological remains are sometimes permitted. There are free public slipways at Carrick and Athlone and dry docks at Richmond Harbour and Killaloe; several hire operators also have slipways. There are drinking-water taps at many public quays.

The Admiralty chart for Lough Derg is no 5080 and for Lough Ree is no 5078. The soundings on the chart for Lough Ree are related to the old Athlone lock, superseded in the 1840s improvements; but they approximate to normal summer level, when there is 7ft of water over the sill of the existing lock. Those of Lough Derg are related to the sill of the lock at Killaloe as explained on the chart. The water level was raised slightly when Ardnacrusha power station was built. Copies of these charts with the navigation markers inserted are displayed beside Athlone Lock; they may also be displayed at Lanesborough and Portumna for Loughs Ree and Derg respectively.

The half-inch to the mile scale Ordnance Survey maps which cover the Shannon Navigation are nos 7, 12, 15, 18 and 17, the latter including only a short section below Killaloe. The one inch to the mile Ordnance Survey maps which cover the navigation as far south as Killaloe are sheets 66, 67, 78, 88, 98, 108, 117, 116, 125 and 134. The one-inch map has not yet been revised to include the post-Ardnacrusha course below Killaloe.

There have been several books of charts and navigational instructions for the Shannon published during the past twenty years—all are at the time of writing either out of date or out of print: the best still available is the set of charts and navigational pilot published by Irish Shell and BP Ltd and originally included in the *Shannon Guide*. Lakes above Lanesborough have been surveyed by Bord Failte or the Board of Works and it is to be hoped that the results will soon be published, for there are no charts available which show soundings for these lakes and visitors are virtually confined to the navigation channels. But what the Shannon really needs is not so much further proliferation of charts as one really good series kept up to date and reprinted annually.

ATHLONE TO ARDNACRUSHA

Since no one starts a Shannon cruise at Battlebridge and few at Ardnacrusha, it seems reasonable to start the gazetteer midway, at Athlone, and work first downstream, and then up.

Athlone (population 9,600, early closing Thursday) is the largest town on the non-tidal Shannon. (See strip map 1, p 131.) Most of the town is on the east bank; the post office and railway station on the west. From the quay on the east bank below the bridge, elegant Edwardian steamers used to depart, full of elegant Edwardian tourists bound for Lough Derg; today it is still a convenient place to start a cruise. On the opposite bank is another quay, and behind it is Athlone Castle which dates from 1210. Immediately downstream are the weir and the lock, which is adjacent to the west bank.

Below the lock the river is in the country. It contains many islands: when approaching them it is important to watch for markers which indicate the navigation course. This is often neither the widest nor the straightest channel. Some miles and several islands downstream, a range of low hills appears ahead—at their western extremity is a cluster of angled roofs and round towers. This is **Clonmacnois**—in the dark and middle ages a great monastic city and seat of learning. A new jetty enables its extensive remains to be visited, and a good descriptive leaflet is available on the spot.

The bridge which gives **Shannonbridge** its name has 16 arches and a navigation span next the east bank. Boats coming down stream through it should beware of others emerging from the quay, which is set back into the bank immediately below it. The navigation span has a temporary Bailey bridge superimposed on it: its rattles, as vehicles cross, could give crews of boats moored here sleepless nights. As at most Shannonside villages and towns, there is no waterfront: the village, probably from fear of floods, retreats from the river and lines the road which aproaches along a ridge of higher ground from the east.

Below Shannonbridge a short artificial cut avoids a hairpin bend in the main channel; opposite the latter the tributary River Suck enters on the west side. It is possible to moor to the banks of the cut. Further on, on the east bank, is Shannonbridge turf-burning power station. A new concrete bridge, built in 1968, spans the river here to carry light railway trains which feed the power station with turf. (See strip map 2, p 132.)

At the approach to the entrance to the Grand Canal near **Shannon Harbour** a backwater diverges to the east. It is not navigable, although it would lead to the canal. Boats heading for the canal must continue past a small island and then turn back into the channel which leads to the canal. They pass the other end of the backwater and the mouth of the Brosna River to port before reaching the canal's 36th lock, and can moor to the bank below the lock.

Banagher has a new marina on the east bank, another multi-arched bridge with rattling Bailey bridge navigation span next the east bank and old quays upstream and downstream of it. The town (early closing Thursday) is on the east bank; its inhabitants have, perhaps, taken to heart Rolt's criticisms in *Green and Silver*, for it is now a tidy well-kept place with most services, and has a pottery by the bridge.

Three-quarters of a mile below Banagher the channel veers sharply to port past Inishee—a tempting, wide, stretch of river straight on is not the navigation. At the end of Inishee it passes between a couple of small islands and then to the west of more large islands. At the end of these is Meelick weir on the west bank, with a strong current above it, and the channel enters the short artificial cut which leads to Victoria Lock, Meelick.

Below the lock the river continues with many large islands until **Portumna** bridge comes into view; its swing span, adjacent to the west bank, is at first hidden by a bend in the bank. Before the bridge is a quay, and the entrance to a short canal which leads to a snug harbour, from which the town is $\frac{3}{4}$ mile further down the road; although there is drinking water at the harbour and fuel close by. The swing span of the bridge, which must be opened for cruisers, is operated by a bridge keeper; there is an inlet on the west bank below the bridge where craft coming upstream can moor until it is ready.

Just over a mile downstream the river enters Lough Derg. (See map on p 44.) Craft coming up the lake here must be careful to turn northwards into the river instead of continuing straight into Terryglass Bay, although the Admiralty chart shows that in most of the bay there is 12 to 14ft of water. On the lake it is important to watch that cross winds do not cause you to drift on to Gortmore and other points. A black warehouse, prominent from the distance, is a good landmark for **Kilgarvan**; there is a sheltered quay behind it and a more exposed one in front, but no village. There is a dilapidated quay in **Rossmore** Bay.

A large red buoy, in the middle of the lake between Rinharra and Curraghmoore Points has been installed as a guide mark. The Benjamin Rocks are one of the trouble spots of Derg: it is better to keep to the east of them and their markers, unless in bad weather the shelter of the west shore of the lake is needed, in which event the more complicated channel west of the rocks can be used. Two beacons in this region are (1969) surmounted by marble busts—they were placed there, I am told, by some young men who possessed busts of their ancestors 'surplus to requirements' and felt that there was no better place to put them.

Dromineer shows up in the distance as a castle and small village on the shore of the lake. A new 300ft jetty gives shelter on its eastern side and berthage both sides. The main

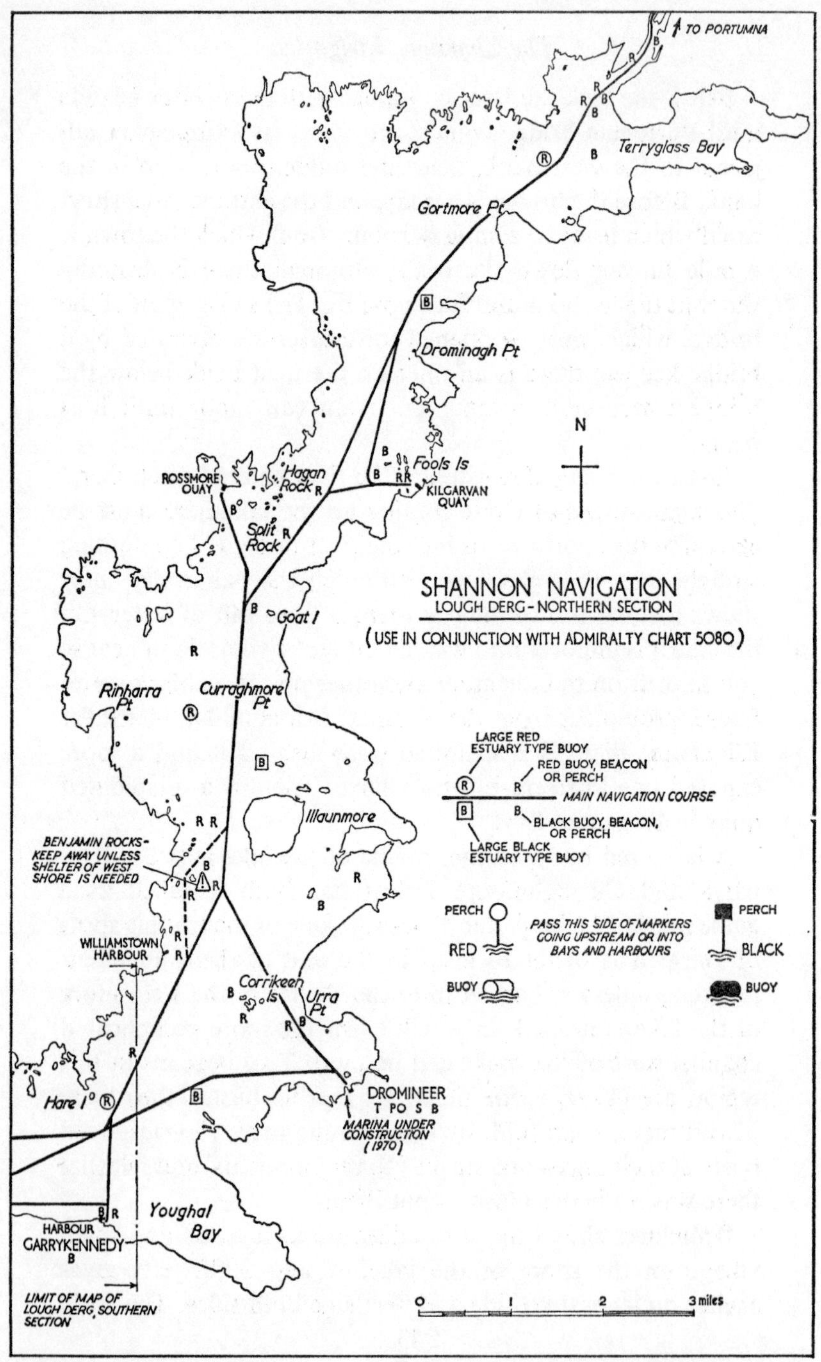

Based on the Ordnance Survey by permission of the Government (Permit No 1427)

part of the village is a couple of hundred yards up the road from the dilapidated quay (fallen stonework under water) by the castle.

The area between Hare Island and Parker Point is notorious for the roughest seas in Lough Derg, particularly when the wind blows from the west down Scarriff Bay. A large ruined tower is a good landmark for the pleasant sheltered harbour of **Garrykennedy**; caution is needed when entering on a following wind. (See map on p 46.) **Mountshannon** also is an attractive place; the village with its tree-lined street is about ¼ mile up the road to the right from the quay. At the entrance to Scarriff Bay is the Middle Ground shoal, another danger point. It is marked, logically enough, by black markers to the south and red markers to the north; this means there is a channel south and north of the markers, but not between them. Holy Island or Inis Cealtra has a round tower and numerous ecclesiastical remains; there is a quay for rowing boats.

The perches marking the entrance to the Scarriff River I found difficult to spot against the afternoon sun. This winding and pleasant little river is navigable for about 1½ miles. The road approach to **Tuamgraney** quay is being restored so that the quay can again be used. Just short of **Scarriff** the river forks: the navigation channel takes the left fork to Scarriff quay. The centre of the town is about ½ mile from the quay, up the lane and then right over the bridge.

To go to Killaloe there is a channel marked between Lushing Rocks and Scilly Island, but there is also deep water between Scilly Island and Parker Point. Crow Island is more conspicuous than its size on the chart suggests. Most of this southern arm of the lake is deep. The approach to **Killaloe** is shown on strip map 3, p 132; the harbour, and fuelling point of Cruising Craft (Shannon) Ltd are on the east bank, and near them is the Lakeside Hotel. Opposite is the entrance to the Killaloe canal, which forms sheltered moorings.

Since for much of its length the canal is separated from the

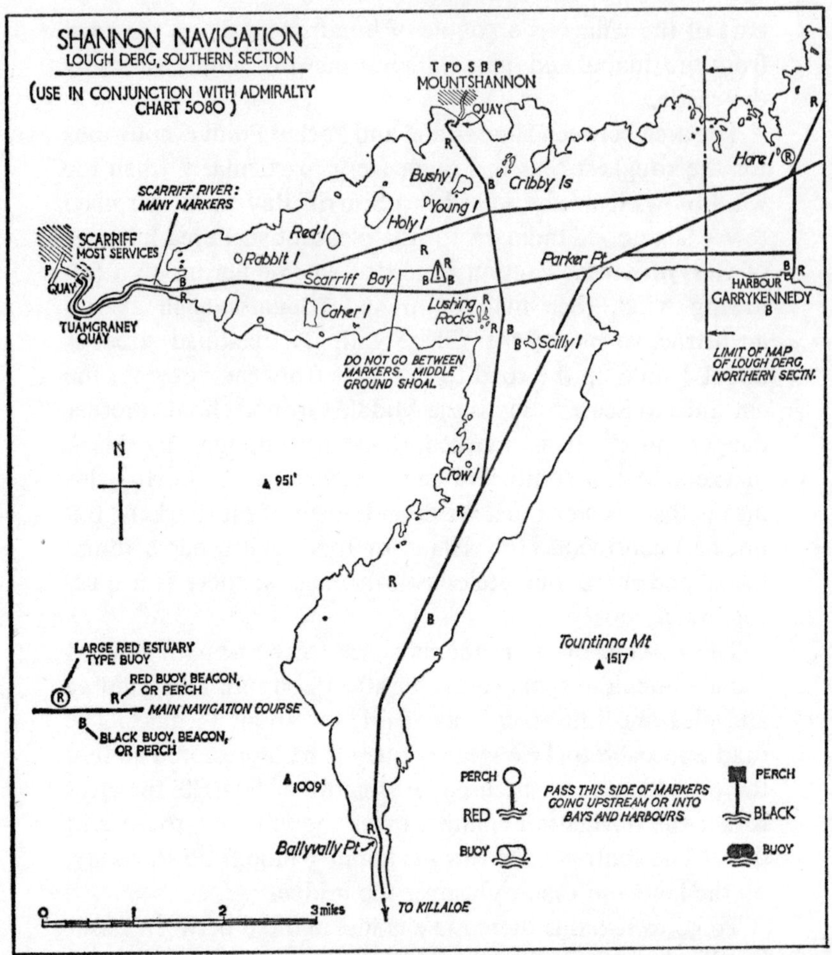

Based on the Ordnance Survey by permission of the Government (Permit No 1427)

river by only a low wall, with the water level the same both sides, its purpose is not obvious. But there used to be a weir in the river downstream of the canal entrance; when Ardnacrusha power station was built, the water right through Killaloe was raised to a uniform level and the weir submerged —it is now marked by buoys. The canal is the start of the former route to Limerick.

Killaloe is surrounded by gorse-covered hills. The town itself is set on a hill, on the west bank of the river, which offers good views back to Lough Derg. On the opposite bank of the river is the village of Ballina. Visitors going downstream should first seek navigation advice from the Shannon Navigation office at Killaloe Lock. The channel passes under a steel span inserted in the stone bridge near the east bank. (Other arches are lower and blocked by an eel fishery.) Only when the current through the bridge is too strong is it necessary to use the canal with its lock; the canal rejoins the navigation channel below the bridge. The navigation now enters the flooded section, an artificial lake made when Ardnacrusha power station was built. It is difficult to navigate, for those without local knowledge. Markers are few and submerged obstructions, such as stone walls and gateposts, are many. The channel follows the east shore of this lake (remains of locks on the old canal protrude above water to the west) for about 3½ miles to Parteen. Here are a dam, a weir and, at their western end, a ship's pass or guillotine control gate by which the navigation channel enters the head race canal to the power station. This canal has sloping edges to which it is not possible to moor, and is lined with high banks which obscure any view.

There is a small jetty on the east bank above **Ardnacrusha** power station. It is intended for boats waiting to pass through the lock, but may also be used for boats while crews visit the power station; there are conducted tours on weekdays except Saturdays and also on summer Sundays. The lock is at the east side of the power station—it has guillotine gates and the fall of the upper chamber is no less than 70ft; that of the lower chamber is about 30ft depending on the state of tide in the tail race canal to which it leads. The lock is operated by the ESB but the normal lock fee is payable for a pass to the Shannon Navigation office at Killaloe or Limerick. The lock-keeper is on duty from 8.0 am to 5.0 pm Monday to Friday, and on other days if 24 hours' notice is given. The water falls and rises fast in the lock chambers and there are vertical rows of steel pegs set in the walls to put ropes round, one after the other.

A full description of the tidal waterway below Ardnacrusha is out of place here, but it may help visitors by sea to mention that the tail race canal, a rushing mass of swirling eddies when the power station is running, is a calm backwater when it is not; and that at **Limerick** the navigation follows a backwater called the Abbey River, spanned by two bridges (Mathew Bridge and Balls Bridge) under which there is inadequate depth of water at low tide, inadequate headroom at high tide and a strong current at other times. Detailed instructions for passage between Ardnacrusha and Limerick docks are supplied by the Board of Works on request, which should state the leading dimensions of the vessel.

UPSTREAM FROM ATHLONE

The navigation span of Athlone road bridge—about which there was so much agitation a few years ago—is adjacent to the west bank. (See strip map 1, p 131.) On the same bank is the church of Saints Peter and Paul, the twin towers of which are landmarks from a long way up and down stream. At Athlone railway bridge the channel passes under the western span. Above it on the east bank is a new harbour and the Jolly Mariner, and new a musical hostelry. About a mile further on on the same bank at Shancurragh is the refuelling point and hire base of Athlone Cruisers Ltd.

The navigation then enters Lough Ree. This lake is shorter than Derg, but, at its southern end, wider. It has fewer harbours in which to take refuge from rough seas, but in fair weather it is equally attractive, particularly when, as I first saw it, the sun blazes down and the water stretches smooth away as far as the eye can reach. Ree lacks surrounding hills, but many islands (notably Inchcleraun) have extensive ecclesiastical remains.

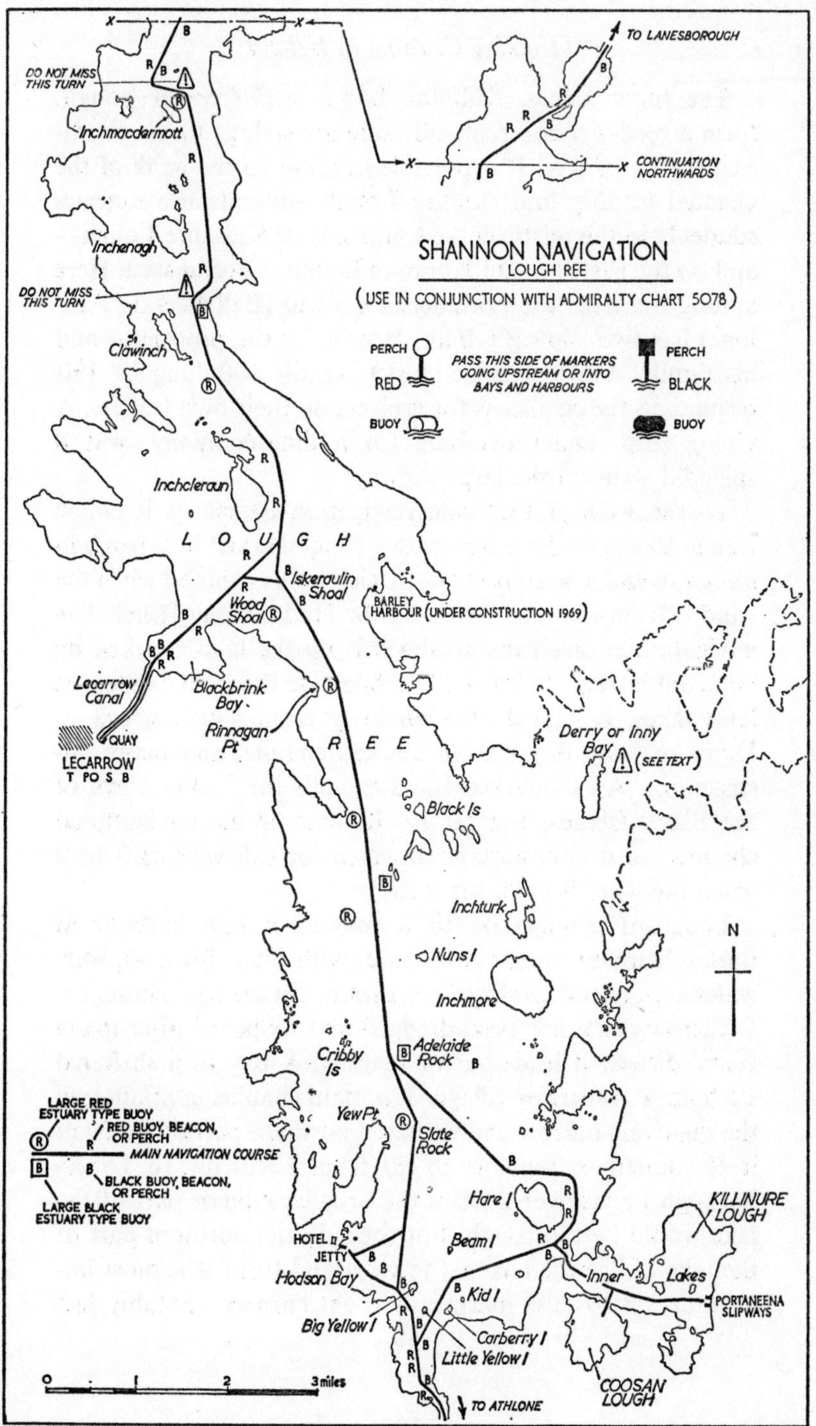

Based on the Ordnance Survey by permission of the Government (Permit No 1427)

The Inner Lakes, Killinure Lough and Coosan Lough, form a reed-girt and reputedly safe appendage to the south-east corner of Ree. It is possible to moor to the bank of the channel leading into Coosan Lough—its entrance appears suddenly in the reeds on the south side of Killinure Lough—and on the east shore of Killinure Lough is **Portaneena**. Here among the trees the Portaneena Co Ltd (Ballykeeran, Athlone) has two slipways, built, largely, by the proprietor and his family; the bigger has a steel cradle 60ft long by 19ft beam, and the smaller is for cruisers on their own trailers. A viking ship, under overhaul for a film company, was a splendid sight on the large slipway.

To the west of the main navigation course as it enters Lough Ree is Hodson Bay, with a shoal marked by a perch in its centre and a landing stage—which looks exposed when the wind is from the east—close by the Hodson Bay Hotel. The navigation course runs northwards up the lake, marked by large but infrequent buoys. The Adelaide Rock, like others in Irish lakes, is named after an early yacht which struck it. Derry or Inny Bay has no marked channel and many obstructions. An unmarked shoal extends for ½ mile north of the Black Islands, not far to the east of the navigational channel, so it is important to watch for sideways drift here when the wind is from the west.

Longford county council is making a new harbour at **Barley Harbour** on the east shore, with plans for a slipway, water supply and, perhaps, restaurant. On the west shore, the Lecarrow canal has been dredged and reopened after many years' disuse. It leads out of Blackbrink Bay to a sheltered harbour at **Lecarrow** village. The main channel continues up the relatively narrow and sheltered northern part of the lake: it is sometimes possible to go from Lecarrow to Lanesborough or vice versa when the broad southern part of the lake would be too rough. But rocks in the northern part of the lake oblige the channel to twist and turn: it is most important not to miss markers and cut corners—notably just

Page 51 Grand Canal: (*above*) Georgian Dublin—the Circular Line; (*right*) rural Ireland—the Barrow Line. The boat is starting to ascend the lower chamber of 24th Lock (double). The lock-keeper has hoisted the racks of the left-hand middle gate. Water is entering through the sluices below, to flow across to the right hand side of the lock and hold the boat snug to the left

Page 52 (*above*) River Barrow Navigation at Graiguenamanagh, looking north to the bridge from the entrance to the lock cut. On the left is a typical Barrow open L-shaped weir, difficult to spot when coming downstream. There is a quay on the right of this picture, but a better one beyond the bridge on the opposite bank. The second arch from the right is marked for navigation; (*below*) Grand Canal system. Typical rack gear at a lock. To operate the gate racks it is necessary to stand on the footboard, which is loose (and avoid tripping over the chains which hold it in position!). Not all locks have land racks like this one

north of Inchmacdermott. The Admiralty chart does not show accurately the approach to Lanesborough, nor the river north to Tarmonbarry—both have been improved since the survey. (The river is shown on strip map 4, p 133.)

At **Lanesborough** bridge the navigation arch (with noisy Bailey bridge over) is adjacent to the west bank and there are quays immediately upstream and downstream of it. There is sometimes a strong current here, and there is little depth of water opposite the quays, so that boats coming downstream and intending to moor are recommended to continue for 200yd or so into the lake before turning to moor against the current. A notice placed on the bridge by the Irish Charter Boat Association advises downstream boats, in uncertain weather, to wait and cross Lough Ree in company. A short distance upstream of the quays, on the same bank, is a small harbour, which pre-dates the 1840s improvements: it is now badly silted. Both quays and harbour are, properly speaking, in Ballyleague, the name of the village on the west bank; Lanesborough itself, a small town with most facilities, is on the east bank.

There is a turf-burning power station on the east bank just upstream of Lanesborough; a bridge for a light railway which feeds this power station crosses the river at Kilnacarrow. The navigation span is marked, and can be raised by Bord na Mona, though this is seldom necessary. Between Lanesborough and Tarmonbarry the navigation channel includes seven cuttings excavated in the bed of the river to give adequate depth; but although there are no less than 50 markers in this section, navigation is still difficult when the water level is low—that is, when there is less than 5ft of water over the lower sill of Tarmonbarry lock, as shown by a scale marked on one of the deep gates.

At the approach to **Tarmonbarry** lock the main navigation course turns northwards round a red perch set well over to the east of the river: straight ahead is the entrance to an artificial cut, which leads through **Clondra** lock to the Camlin

River. The lock, disused for some years, is to be reopened in 1970; it is 18ft wide and 82ft long. To turn right at the end of the cut leads, in a few yards, to the tail of another lock on the far bank; beyond is a weir. The lock rises to **Richmond Harbour** and its dimensions are 14ft 6in by 75ft. The harbour, restored after ten years of disuse, was the terminus of the Royal Canal, now abandoned, which used to extend from here to Dublin. Beside it is the hamlet of Cloondara (or Cloondra, or Clondra: spelling of names is imprecise hereabouts). To turn left at the end of the cut leads up the Camlin River, which eventually re-enters the Shannon at the south end of Lough Forbes. This was the navigation channel prior to the 1840s improvements and, with the reopening of Clondra lock, becomes an alternative route; it is narrow, winding, overhung by bushes and sometimes weedy, but it has been dredged in places, and the banks are often soft enough to moor to.

The main channel continues upstream through **Tarmonbarry** (or Termonbarry) lock. There are quays on the west bank below and above the lock, which is itself separated from the east bank by the weir, to which boats coming downstream are rather exposed. The navigation span of Tarmonbarry bridge adjoins the west bank; it has only 9ft headroom, but can be raised by the bridge keeper to give 16ft 6in. Red lights which shine up and down stream from the bridge, and cause strangers some confusion, indicate only that the lifting span is lowered: boats able to pass under the span when lowered do so against the lights. To have either Tarmonbarry or Roosky (qv) bridges raised, the lock-keeper at the previous lock encountered should be advised. A small quay has recently been built on the west bank upstream from the bridge; the village lines the road away from the bridge on the same side.

From Tarmonbarry to Lough Forbes the bed and banks of the river are frequently rocky. The eastern shores of Lough Forbes, a pleasant small lake, are covered in woods, in contrast to the open country to the west. The navigation channel follows the west bank, which itself turns to the west about 1½ miles from the south end of the lake. Shore outlines, as shown on maps, are obscured by reed beds, particularly to the east; the Bord Failte chart shows that in open water, away from shores and reed beds, there is generally at least 6ft depth over a mud bottom—but the entrance to Castle Bay, where Forbes is written on the half-inch map, is obstructed by rocks. The Rinn River enters through reeds near the northernmost point of the lake and is best found by keeping to the navigation channel until it opens up on the opposite shore; its mouth is shoal to a depth of about 2ft, but craft which can cross this can navigate as far as **Cloonart** bridge. Holland Supercraft, in 1969 at Roosky, plan to establish a hire base here and to dredge the mouth of the river. The main channel continues up a wide stretch of river to **Roosky** lock, see map on p 56.

This lock adjoins the east bank of the river; there are small quays on this bank above and below it. The weir is west of the lock; there is sometimes a strong flow towards it from upstream. Roosky (Rooskey, Ruskey) is ½ mile above the lock; there are quays and waterside fuelling points on both banks. The navigation span of the bridge is next the east bank; its headroom is 11ft, but it can be raised by the bridge keeper to give 18ft of headroom if necessary; once again there are red lights shining up and down stream, to be ignored by all except those few who need the bridge raised. There is no quay upstream of the bridge.

Roosky village by day appears a small, drab, deserted place, devoid of interest except for Hanley's bacon factory—from its shop, ½ mile down the road west of the bridge, I have obtained succulent pork chops and gammon. But such is the Irish temperament that Roosky by night shows more gaiety than an English town ten times the size, and its pubs, such as the Crew's Inn, and dance hall abound with rhythmical music and song.

Three-quarters of a mile upstream of Roosky the river

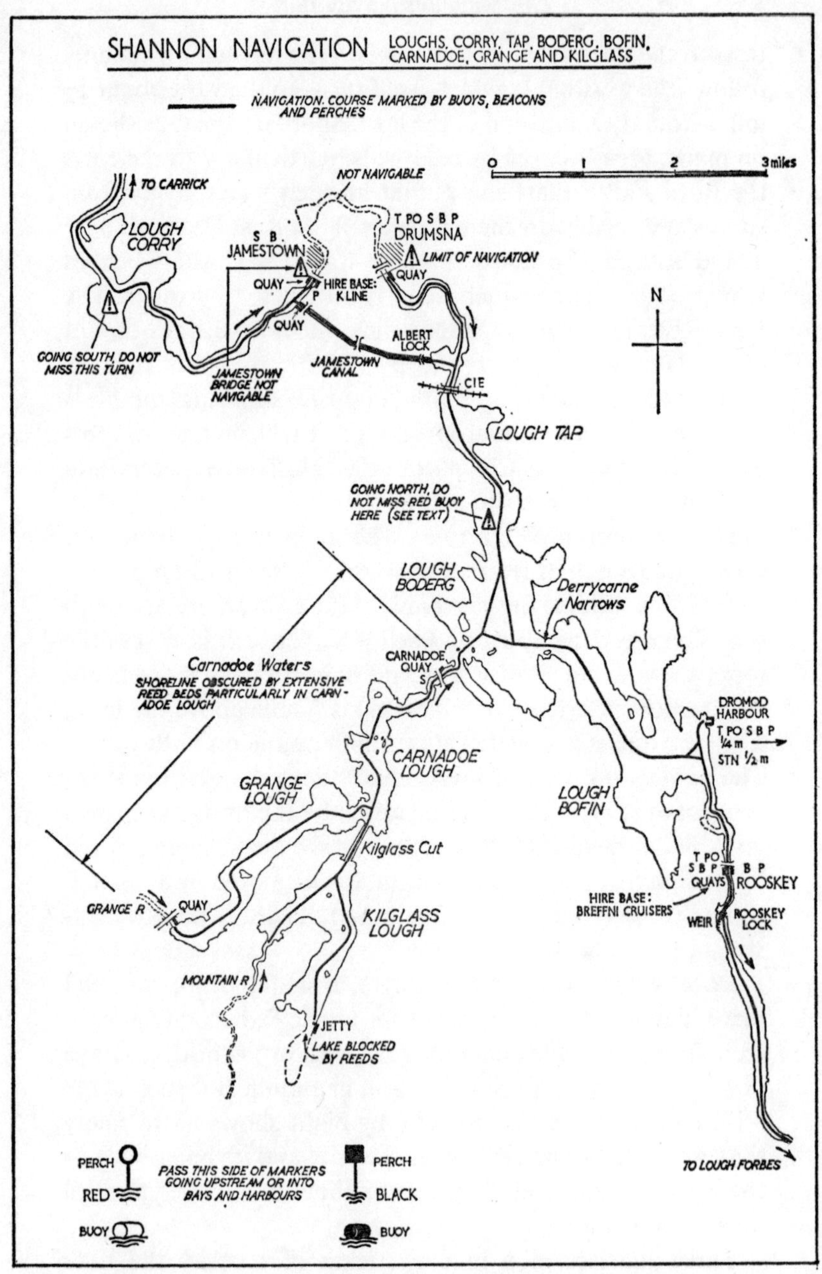

Based on the Ordnance Survey by permission of the Government (Permit No 1427)

enters Lough Bofin. The harbour of **Dromod** (Drumod, Dromad) lies ahead on the east shore; there are rocks immediately beyond it, and a right-angled turn to starboard at the entrance, so that it is difficult to enter or leave when the wind is from the south-west with a fetch of 1¼ miles across the lake. Once inside, it is pleasant, sheltered and recently improved by lowering the quays to suit cruisers. The village is about ¼ mile up the road.

The main navigation channel, on entering Bofin, bears west, and then north between wooded shores; the southward extension of the lake, though not part of the navigation channel, appears from the Board of Works chart to be clear of obstructions outside the reed line. The main channel, as it approaches the head of the lake, bears west again through the Derrycarne Narrows—rocky, but well marked—to enter Lough Boderg. Both Bofin and Boderg are large enough to be uncomfortably choppy at times.

In Lough Boderg, the main navigation course leads northwards again, but on the west shore, a little too far north to be described as opposite Derrycarne, is the entrance to Carnadoe. This channel leads straight between three pairs of perches and then, just as a bridge comes into view beyond the water straight ahead, makes a sudden S-bend to port. **Carnadoe** (Carranadoe) quay, with stacks of reeds for thatching, is just before the bridge.

Beyond the bridge commence the Carnadoe Waters, a chain of lakes between low hills where women spread washing out to dry on thorn bushes and men drive by on donkey carts singing at the tops of their voices—or did, when I was there—and where a reputable hire operator claims to have met a mermaid in the reeds! These lakes are said to be free of rocks and their edges are fringed with reed beds which obscure the shore. The reed beds are particularly extensive in Carnadoe Lough, the first of the lakes, and the marked channel twists and turns between them—at one point they divide the lake in two and the narrow channel is cut through the reeds. At the south end of Carnadoe Lough the channel turns west through the reeds to Grange Lough, at the further extremity of which the Grange River is navigable for about 50yd to a quay on its north bank which has road access but no facilities. Also leading out of the south end of Carnadoe Lough is the artificial Kilglass Cut to Kilglass Lough. The western arm of this lake leads to the Mountain River, navigable for about a mile with banks to which it is possible to moor, and the eastern arm to a very dilapidated jetty in shallow water at its south end—skippers of large cruisers would probably do well to reconnoitre by dinghy before attempting to come alongside. The lake beyond is blocked by reeds.

To return to the main course through Lough Boderg: it is important not to miss the first red buoy which marks the start of the channel north out of the lake: boats which have missed it have gone on the rocks at the north-west corner. The navigation channel then leads through a short river section, a small lake (Lough Tap), and under the bridge carrying the Mullingar–Carrick–Sligo railway. It turns to the west upstream of the bridge, to Albert Lock, but the main stream of the river continues straight on, then follows a curving reach to **Drumsna** (stress the second syllable); it is navigable to a quay on the east bank. The village is neat but small. Upstream of the quay the river is not navigable and there is a stretch of rapids.

These are avoided by the artificial Jamestown Canal entered through Albert Lock; it is narrow by Shannon standards, and a bridge on a blind corner half-way along it requires caution. Where the canal rejoins the river is a rural quay on the west bank, and the main navigation course turns to the left upstream. The river is also navigable to the right downstream (so leave black marker to port) for a few hundred yards to **Jamestown**, at the approach to which place is a rocky shoal with some 3ft depth of water over it. There is a public quay to port as you approach, and K line's hire base, with waterside fuel supply, opposite; the bridge is not navigable.

Upstream from the mouth of the Jamestown Canal the main navigation course winds its way through the several expansions of the river that collectively form Lough Corry. (Easy to miss a turning here.) The Bord Failte chart for these little lakes shows no unmarked obstructions away from shore and reed line, but the shores of lake and river are in places rocky. On the east bank between Lough Corry and Carrick on Shannon is **Rosebank Marina**, the base of Flag Line, with waterside fuelling point. An island in midstream separates it from the main channel. (See strip map 5, p 133.)

Carrick on Shannon (early closing Wednesday), though with a population of only 1,500, is the capital of the north Shannon and has shops and hotels to meet most boaters' needs. The first and third arches of the bridge from the east bank are marked for navigation and the old quay extends both sides of the bridge on the east bank. Upstream on the west bank is a new quay and opposite it on the east bank extensive new marina developments.

About 1½ miles above Carrick the Boyle River enters from the west. The Shannon continues wide as far as Hartley Bridge, and then narrows. A canal which enters on the east bank is navigable for ¼ mile to a quay on its south bank at **Leitrim**, a small and pleasant village. The canal was the start of the Ballinamore & Ballyconnell Canal, opened through to the Erne in 1860 as part of a waterway link between the Shannon and Belfast and disused since 1869. There is much talk of restoring it for pleasure cruising.

There is no room for large craft such as barges to turn at Leitrim, so they must go back to the Shannon astern; at the mouth of the canal they are protected from the current by an underwater wall between the bank and an island in the river —so boats going upstream must pass west of the island. The river continues to be navigable as far as the tail of **Battlebridge** lock on the east bank. Upstream the river shoals immediately. The lock is impassable, but used to give access to the Lough Allen Canal, which led to the lake of that name but is now closed. There are thoughts of reopening it too. There is no village at Battlebridge, but there is a small shop reached by following the canal towpath to the first bridge and turning left down the road.

The Boyle River with several lakes on its course is an attractive cruising ground—in March sunshine, when snow still lingered on mountains to the north, it was very attractive indeed. The first lake is Lough Eidin or Drumharlow, which though inviting does have some unmarked hazards off the marked course, followed by a short section of river and the small Cootehall Lough. At **Cootehall** the marked navigation channel is excavated through rock in the river bed and passes under the arch of the bridge next to the south bank. On the north bank are successively the hire base of Shannon Cruisers Ltd, and the public quay, next the bridge—but a ridge of rock along the centre of the river separates deep water off the

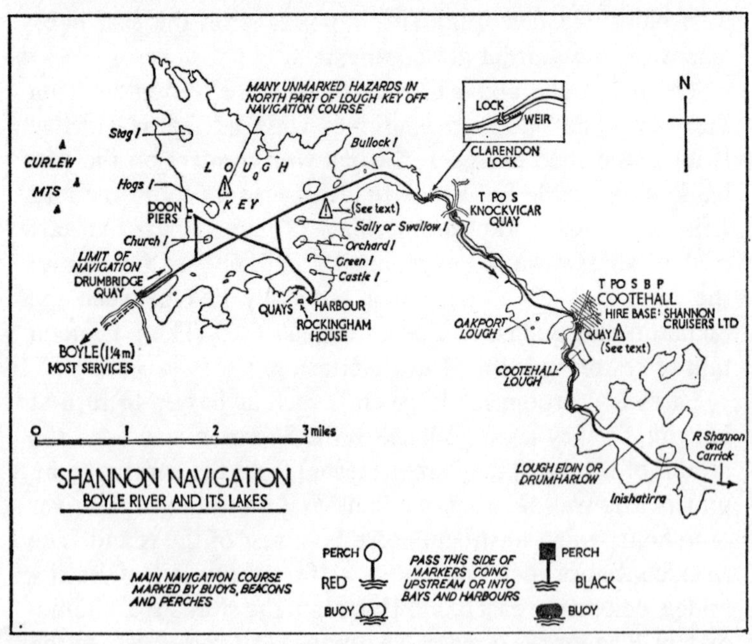

Based on the Ordnance Survey by permission of the Government (Permit No 1427)

quay from the navigation channel and craft aiming for or leaving the quay must diverge from or regain the navigation channel downstream of the second of two black perches below the bridge, which mark the rock. Probably, improvements of the 1840s were left incomplete here.

Upstream from Cootehall is Oakport Lough, which the Bord Failte chart indicates is free from underwater obstructions away from islands, reed line and shores—the eastern shore in particular is rocky in places. More river leads to **Knockvicar**, with quay, on the north bank, and bridge. By it lives the lock-keeper for Clarendon Lock, which is 800yd upstream next to the north bank, and gives access to Lough Key.

Lough Key is the scenic climax to a cruise up the Shannon; its islands and promontories, covered in woods and topped by castles, have the Curlew Mountains to the west as a backdrop. And the climax to Lough Key is Rockingham House, set on its hill above the south shore; it was designed by Nash with a refinement that triumphs over its wild surroundings. But Rockingham is only a shell, for it was burnt a few years ago. Now there is a plan to demolish even the shell and replace it by a hilltop museum, all part of a greater and otherwise admirable plan for 'Lough Key Forest Park'. Even in its present ruined state, Rockingham catches the imagination of those who first see it from the water, and it would be a very brilliant architect who designed a replacement as superb in its setting. Perhaps it would be possible to retain at least that façade which faces the lake.

Navigationally, Lough Key is not so good. The bottom is poor holding ground for anchors, the weather often variable, and there are many unmarked hazards, so that those without local knowledge would be ill-advised to stray from the main navigation courses. These lead to Rockingham, Doon and Drum Bridge. Note particularly that the course to **Rockingham** passes west of the red buoy off Sally Island: many boats have gone on the rocks from trying to cut this corner by passing between Sally and Orchard or Orchard and Green Islands. At Rockingham two small quays in front of the house are exposed, and shallow, with fallen stonework beneath the water, but the harbour in the corner of the bay south-east of the house is sheltered and has road access. At **Doon** two concrete piers, which are rather exposed, have sufficient depth of water at their ends for cruisers to moor, but a third, the most northerly, does not. They are used by swimmers. The **Drum Bridge** course follows the Boyle River for about ½ mile beyond the lake; the navigation ends at a low bridge which appears suddenly round a right-hand bend. There is a quay on the north bank, and the town of **Boyle** is 1¼ miles up the road.

CHAPTER THREE

The Grand Canal[1]

If the predominant impression of the lower Shannon is one of remoteness from human habitation and activity, that of the Grand Canal is the opposite. Its surroundings—farms, fields, lanes, hedgerows—close in on it and the canal seeks out such towns and villages as there are. There is more to see from the canal.

Alongside it is the evidence of the last 200 years and more of Irish history—grand country houses, neat thatched and whitewashed cottages, the elegance of Georgian Dublin and the earnest drabness of tenement-replacing blocks of flats. There are slowly shrinking peat bogs from which the turf is cut by hand and carried away by donkey cart, and science fiction cooling towers of turf-burning power stations set starkly in similar bogs which are being shrunk much more quickly by machine. There are ruined castles past which the canal flows fortuitously and former hotels purposely built on its quays by the Grand Canal Company for passenger traffic which now seems almost as remote as the wars for which the castles were constructed.

The canal comprises the Main Line, 26 miles from Dublin to Lowtown; the Shannon Line, 53 miles from Lowtown to Shannon Harbour, with a branch of 1 mile to Edenderry (the Main and Shannon Lines together are often called the 'Main Line'); the Barrow Line, 28½ miles from Lowtown to Athy; and the Circular Line, 3¾ miles through Dublin to Ringsend

[1] See pages 134 to 137 for Grand Canal strip maps.

Docks. All other former branches are now closed. There are 19 locks on the Main Line, including 4 double locks; of these 11, including 3 double, are concentrated in 4½ miles on the outskirts of Dublin. (In Ireland a lock with two successive chambers separated by a single pair of gates—that is, a riser or staircase in English terms—is called a double lock: it counts as one in the numbering of locks and only one lock fee is payable.) There are 17 locks, including 1 double lock, on the Shannon Line; none on the Edenderry Branch; 9 locks including 2 double locks on the Barrow Line; 7 locks on the Circular Line and 3 parallel tide locks of various sizes, at Ringsend. Here the canal joins the tidal River Liffey; at Shannon Harbour it joins the Shannon Navigation; and at Athy it joins the River Barrow Navigation. The latter is included, administratively, in the Grand Canal system; but since in practice it is a very different sort of waterway I have given it a separate chapter.

Most of the Grand Canal was built between 1756 and 1805. It belonged to the Grand Canal Company from 1772 until 1950, when the company was amalgamated with CIE. The Grand Canal is the sole survivor of Irish canal systems, and there has been no trade on it for ten years. There is a proposal to transfer it from CIE to the Office of Public Works. The Main Line west of 12th Lock, near Lucan, and the Shannon Line are reasonably well maintained, considering the lack of traffic; the Barrow Line is more weedy and overgrown; and the section from 12th Lock down to Dublin and Ringsend, which has been under threat of closure since 1963, is in poor condition.

CIE plans no major improvements to the canal, although there are signs of a few detailed improvements. Lock gates are to be replaced, probably at a rate of two a year. Rubbish bins have been provided at some of the locks and applicants for lock permits are now issued also with a pamphlet giving details of the navigation. There are now four mechanical weed cutters.

Weed is inevitably a problem on the Grand Canal, as on all little used canals. *Holiday Cruising on Inland Waterways* devotes page 62 to what boaters should do about it, and on the Grand Canal it is also desirable to check and clean the water intake filter of your boat at least twice a day. Where weed cutters are in operation there is often much weed floating on the surface and maintenance crews sometimes stretch a rope across the canal to prevent its floating away. The rope is difficult to spot, so that it is as well to check any particularly dense patch of floating weed before attempting to plough through it: otherwise the result is a cut rope wedged solidly round your propeller, a state of affairs satisfactory neither to CIE nor yourself!

The maximum permitted dimensions for boats to navigate the canal are: overall length—61ft; beam—13ft; height above water line—9ft; draught—4ft. Maximum draught is often reduced to 3ft 6in during dry summers. Before navigating the canal, craft require a lock permit, obtainable at a fee of 2s 3d (probably to be 11p) a lock from: CIE Canal Section, Civil Engineering Department, Pearse Station, Dublin 2; Canal Depot, Tullamore, Co Offaly; or the lock-keepers at Shannon Harbour, Carlow or Graiguenamanagh (the latter two places being on the River Barrow Navigation). The skipper may be required to sign an indemnity. Each boat must carry a number or name by which it can be identified.

CIE requires sufficient people on each boat to manage it competently. The maximum speed permitted is 4mph, to prevent damage to the canal banks. In strong cross winds, steering in the confined width of the canal becomes a skilled job, particularly when the canal is on an embankment, and when a boat is moving slowly towards a lock.

All Grand Canal locks have lock-keepers, most of whom control two, three or four locks. Normally they are on duty during daylight on weekdays; they are off duty on Sundays. Lock-keepers are there to operate the locks for any boat who needs them, but CIE has no objection to competent crews working boats through the locks themselves. The method of working locks is described in the pamphlet mentioned above, and is basically the same as that described in pages 78 to 85 of *Holiday Cruising on Inland Waterways*. Some of the terminology is different to that in use on English canals: top gates here are called breast gates, bottom gates are deep gates and a pound, ie the section of canal between two locks, is a level. Sluices are still called paddles, but the term equivalent to 'opening the paddles' is 'opening (or hoisting) the racks', that is the racks of the rack-and-pinion gearing by which the paddles are opened and closed. Ground paddles are referred to as land racks. A windlass, the cranked spanner used to operate the racks, becomes a lock key. (On the Lower Bann Navigation it is called a sluice handle, but this point is of academic interest, for there it is used only by lock-keepers.)

When closing lock gates it is essential to make sure that they mate correctly at the mitre posts in the centre. Failure to ensure that gates were correctly mitred has resulted in their bursting open. There are no locks with single top gates, as on some English narrow canals: all have a pair of breast gates. Most locks have two racks in each gate and some also have a pair of land racks adjacent to the breast gates. But it is common to find locks at which one or more of the racks are out of order.

To operate gate racks, it is usually necessary to stand on foot boards mounted on the gates. These foot boards are loose: the ends tip up if you stand on them and they are held in position by chains neatly placed to trip unwary feet although there are, apparently, no records of accidents from this cause. (The objects of having the foot boards loose are so that they are easily moved to get at obstructions on the sill, and to maintain the paddles; and on deep gates, so that long craft such as barges cannot get caught under them as they rise in the lock.) When a small boat is ascending a lock, it has a less turbulent ride if racks on the side to which it is moored are opened first: the water bursts into the lock at an angle and rushes along the opposite side. There are no chains, or anything to hold on to, on the sides of lock chambers, but there are usually posts positioned more or less conveniently beside each lock and it is always easier to hold a boat in position by its mooring rope if a turn is taken round one of these. Below locks, the absence of any convenient place to join or leave boats remains as conspicuous as it was when Rolt commented on it in *Green and Silver* in 1949, but provision of such landing places is being investigated.

A Grand Canal lock key is a more substantial thing than an English windlass. A typical one, with a square at both ends, measures 15in overall along one arm of the L and 12in along the other. (Typical English windlasses have a 10½in shank.) With the lock key, the long arm, with more leverage, is used to hoist racks and the shorter one, which can be turned more quickly, to lower them and also to hoist any racks which are particularly free running. Lock keys have been hard to obtain recently and CIE does not issue them. Hire operators supply them with their boats and Croxon & Dobbs Ltd, Ship Chandlers (3 Windmill Lane, Rogerson's Quay, Dublin 2) now stock them. The square measures 1¼in across the flats which suggests that English windlasses of the large type would fit Irish rack gear, but lack of leverage resulting from the short shank would make their continued use hard work.

Boats on the canal must not be moored where they would obstruct the navigation—for instance at locks or bridges. Long-term moorings are available, subject to certain conditions, for £2 4s 3d (probably to be £2.21) a month. There are no slipways on the canal but there are dry docks at Tullamore and Shannon Harbour. Drinking water can be obtained near most locks.

There are still a few barges on the canal, which tend to appear unexpectedly round blind corners. Commercial carrying ceased in 1960—surviving barges are used for maintenance, or converted for pleasure cruising. (CIE says it has no more for sale.) They carry numbers, followed by cryptic initials, of which the origin and meaning are:

M—Grand Canal Company's *M*otor (as opposed to horse-drawn) barge.

E —Grand Canal Company's *E*ngineering department maintenance barge.

B —*B*ye trader's barge, ie owned by an independent trader not by the canal company.

The Grand Canal appears on Ordnance Survey half-inch scale maps sheets 15 and 16, and on one-inch scale maps sheets 108, 109, 110, 111, 112 and 119.

SHANNON LINE, SHANNON HARBOUR TO LOWTOWN

(See strip maps 1–4, pp 134–5.)

The approach from the Shannon to 36th Lock is not straightforward, but is described in the chapter on the Shannon Navigation. 36th and 35th Locks separate the river from **Shannon Harbour** proper; the lock-keeper for these and 34th Lock lives beside 35th Lock. Shannon Harbour is a sad place, full of reminders of commerce and the past that was prosperous not so very long ago. Above 35th Lock most of the width of the canal is spanned by the awning of the transhipment shed that was used to transfer goods from canal barges to larger river and lake barges. (To fit them, 36th and 35th Locks are 16ft wide.) Beyond, on the south bank, runs a row of buildings and houses in varying states of repair which culminates in the classical hulk of the former canal hotel.

Above Shannon Harbour the canal enters a pleasant if undistinguished countryside and passes through 34th Lock. Roads and lanes are carried over it from time to time by humped bridges, finely proportioned arches of grey stone inscribed with their date of construction and name, which usually commemorates landowner, builder or an early Grand Canal Company director. They become familiar along the whole length of the canal.

At **Belmont** is 33rd Lock, a double lock with an inconvenient bridge which spans the lower chamber. Steersmen going through for the first time are well advised to stop and inspect beforehand. To hold boats steady while ascending or descending the lower chamber, the local recommendation is to put both bow and stern lines round a post on the south side of the lock, west of the bridge. The lock-keeper for this and 32nd Lock lives at 32nd Lock.

Beyond 32nd Lock the canal enters a 9 mile long level. At Gallen or Armstrong bridge is a quay, the most convenient for the village of **Ferbane**, a mile to the north. A long stretch of bog follows, in the middle of which the canal crosses over the Silver River by McCartney Aqueduct. At **Pollagh** is a very small village and the only road bridge for several miles. The 31st and 30th Locks come close together with the lock-keeper at the latter; the village of **Rahan** is to the north of the canal between Becans and Corcorans Bridges, and on the south side is The Thatch, a good little pub-cum-shop which appears to be one of the few slate-roofed buildings in the district. The canal crosses the Clodiagh River by Kilgortin Aqueduct and passes the ruins of seventeenth-century Ballycowan castle before reaching 29th Lock with its well tended garden. The lock-keeper for this lock and for 28th Lock (up boats) lives here.

On the outskirts of **Tullamore** are a railway bridge and then 28th and 27th Locks: the lock-keeper at the latter attends to it and to 28th Lock for down boats. A little further on, on the south bank, a notice invites boats to moor to the whiskey distillery quay, where once barge-loads of grain arrived. Alternatively boats continue to the eastern end of the town, and turn sharply to the right under a bridge into the arm which leads, after 50yd and another sharp right turn, to the harbour. This CIE plans to make the headquarters of the maintenance staff. The pleasantest mooring I found was in the harbour approach arm, although there was fallen stonework in the water by the bank which necessitated caution.

Here we whiled away a sunny afternoon, under the trees near another old canal hotel, waiting for a crew member who through no fault of his own did not turn up, watching nuns playing tennis opposite and studying an enormous Mercedes in which a family party of Germans arrived to take out one of Gay Line's hire craft. This hire operator also supplied according to a notice diesel, petrol, oil, water, repairs, toilets and telephone.

Tullamore (early closing Wednesday, population 6,243) is the largest town on the canal outside Dublin. It has banks, hotels, post office and tourist office (among most other facilities) reached by going down the street from the harbour and turning left at the crossroads. The railway station is on the far side of the town, down the road to Roscrea and Birr.

The main line of the canal climbs away from Tullamore by a series of six locks at intervals of from $\frac{1}{4}$ mile to 2 miles. The first of these, 26th Lock, has a relatively large and ornate lock cottage (a contractor appears to have built it this way at his own initiative, and to have met some resistance from the directors of the canal company when he presented his bill). The lock-keeper for 26th, 25th and 24th Locks is Mrs Kelly who lives at 25th Lock and was not averse to joining us on the boat between locks. We were rewarded with a fund of local information of which the story which made the greatest impression on us (and also, evidently, on her) related to an Englishman who, only the previous week, had been obliged to have twenty stitches in his face as a result of a brush with a lock key. The lock-keeper for 23rd, 22nd and 21st Locks lives at 21st Lock.

Above 21st Lock commences the Long Level of $18\frac{3}{4}$ miles. The junction of the closed Kilbeggan branch is just above the lock and a few hundred yards beyond is Chevenix or Ballycommon bridge with a small quay and a pub/shop close by. After a further $3\frac{1}{2}$ miles is the large village of **Daingean** or Philipstown. Then the farms and scrubland through which the canal has passed since Tullamore give way to bog which is being harvested mechanically. The canal is crossed by a lifting bridge (manned by a bridge keeper) used by Bord na Mona light railway trains and turf-cutting machinery. The canal leads on and on: one vista of water, bog, woods and sky succeeds another until the junction with the Edenderry branch is reached.

The branch, which is entered by a sharp turn under a bridge to the north, is about a mile long and in good condition; it leads to the town of **Edenderry** (population 2,690, early closing Thursday). The quay here is a garden, bright and gay with flowers through the enthusiasm, I believe, of the local priest. Visiting boaters are made welcome and asked for their comments and suggestions; their needs, in the way of quayside water supply and rubbish disposal, are met. Edenderry is evidently proud of its canal: the result is an object lesson to other canalside towns.

On the main line, after the junction, come more long straight stretches across the Bog of Allen. The canal is carried on an embankment, with an aqueduct over a main road and fine and extensive views on either side. At the edge of the bog is the isolated 20th Lock, with its lock-keeper living alongside, which gives access to another long level of 7 miles. Above the lock is Ticknevin or Hartley bridge, with quays on both sides of the canal, although that on the south side is overgrown.

After Ticknevin the country becomes less open. The canal passes Lullymore peat briquette factory, where the peat briquettes which are now a familiar fuel were first produced in the thirties. A couple of miles further on is another Bord na Mona light railway lifting bridge; the trains carry turf to Allenwood power station which can be seen ½ mile to the north of the canal. It was the second of the turf-burning stations to be built, commissioned in 1952. At Bond Bridge, the village of **Allenwood** is five minutes' walk to the north. At **Lowtown** the Barrow Line of the canal, described below, enters from the south. There is no village here.

MAIN LINE, LOWTOWN TO DUBLIN
(See strip maps 4–6, pp 135–6.)

The 19th Lock is close beyond the junction; its lock-keeper lives beside it, and above it is the 4-mile long summit level of the canal, 279ft above sea level. Since Allenwood the water has become clear, and it has been possible, from the bows of a boat, to watch shoals of fish swim ahead of it; at 19th Lock the water is so clear that even when the lock is full its bed can be seen. This water comes from a source called Seven Springs down the Milltown Feeder Canal or Grand Supply, which enters the canal immediately above 19th Lock. Westbound boats must turn a corner to the right to find the lock and avoid the feeder, a broad and tempting stretch of water straight ahead. The clarity of the water continues little diminished right down to Ringsend.

Binns' Bridge, Robertstown, is the delight of photographers: from the west the stately pile of the old canal hotel appears framed in its arch. **Robertstown**—shops, pubs, houses, warehouses—groups itself in an arc along the quay on the south bank between bridge and hotel. It is a delightful place, a real canal village and home to many barge men.

The canal leaves Robertstown by a long straight embankment, followed by a cutting through the Hill of Downings. Here it has left the Midland bogs behind and entered the fertile eastern seaboard. The descent starts with 18th, 17th and 16th Locks, all within 1½ miles of one another; their lock-keeper lives near 16th Lock. The River Liffey is crossed by the Leinster Aqueduct, a substantial stone multi-arched structure. Half a mile further on is Soldier's Island at the junction with the closed branch to Naas. At **Sallins** is a busy mill which no doubt owes its location to the canal; there is a quay opposite, but further quays on either side of the canal beyond the bridge would probably be quieter.

Beyond Sallins is a long, winding, leafy cutting; at the end of it the canal passes under the main line railway from Dublin to the south-west, and in another mile comes to 15th Lock. This and 14th Lock are close together, and their lock-keeper lives at 15th Lock where he tends a well kept garden. Below 14th Lock a feeder enters on the south bank with an appreciable current.

The section of canal which follows was one of the earliest to be constructed. Unlike their contemporaries in England, the builders made no attempt to follow the contours of the ground. The canal runs straight, striding across country on long embankments or slicing through long rock cuttings which must in their day have been formidable engineering feats. From the embankments are views to the Wicklow mountains away to the south-east; and in June the canal is lined with fields bright with buttercups and thorn trees snowy with blossom.

Lyons House, a country mansion to be seen to the south of the canal, was the home of Lord Cloncurry, an early director of the Grand Canal Company. The 13th Lock, close by, is a double lock, with resident lock-keeper. At **Hazelhatch** bridge is a quay and a couple of pubs. Just above **Twelfth Lock** is a mill, and a pub with a waterside drinking water-tap. This place is favoured by many as a permanent mooring for cruisers, and it is a good place to pause before descending on Dublin.

Unfortunately the descent into Dublin by canal cannot be recommended for a happy family holiday. Unfortunately, because Dublin is a city well worth a visit: it ought to be possible to visit it by boat as conveniently as by any other means, and certainly more cheaply, considering the prices of its hotels. But despite the difficulties described below, determined and able-bodied waterways enthusiasts should certainly not miss it, and this route remains the simplest access to the Grand Canal/Barrow/Shannon network for people arriving in their own boats by sea. During my visit we passed several other boats.

The snags are:

(*a*) The section is relatively heavily locked (this by itself is no disadvantage to a crew that is not afraid of hard work).

(*b*) The lock gates are in poor condition and the canal in places is shallow.

(*c*) There are no facilities provided for pleasure craft on the canal in Dublin and there appears to be nowhere to moor a boat in confidence that it will not be interfered with if left unattended.

(*d*) Many Dubliners, like their counterparts in English cities, evidently regard the canal as bottomless and therefore a suitable place to dispose of quantities of plastic sacks, old clothes, wooden boxes, large pieces of timber, dead dogs, and unwanted chairs, bicycles, perambulators and motor-cars. Such of these as do not wrap themselves around propellers obstruct the navigation and prevent lock gates being opened fully. CIE is constantly removing rubbish and during the winter of 1968–9 sections of the Circular Line were drained for a noble voluntary clearance effort by members of the IWAI. If more boats used the canal, the locks would be used more often and floating debris could float away downstream.

(*e*) Bands of youths and small boys hinder the passage of boats, get in the way at locks, endanger themselves, and, given the chance, climb on board (we closed and locked the windows). I met no hostility—we were neither stoned nor spat at, as others have reported. But we did meet plenty of mischief: such as swimmers in a lock who endeavoured to climb into our dinghy and half swamped it. But it seemed to me that for every youth who was objectionable, there was another who was helpful. We were ascending 2nd Lock as the inmates of a primary school came out for their midday break: at one stage I counted fifteen of them heaving on a balance beam with me. Considering the magnetic attraction that the canal has for young Dubliners it is surprising that there seem to be no sea scouts or other youth organisations based on it to turn their interest into constructive channels.

In the event of trouble a friendly but firm approach is needed—I have heard it suggested that the solution is to invite obvious ringleaders on board and get them, and their gangs, to work for you. Probably the best solution of all is to arrange your visit when children are otherwise occupied in school. And, of course, the more boats that pass along the canal, the less interest they will arouse.

It is a day's journey from 12th Lock to Ringsend. Before leaving it is a good thing to ensure that your engine is entirely reliable, and to check with CIE that there are no unexpected stoppages, for there is nowhere convenient to leave a boat further down. 12th Lock has a resident lock-keeper and is deep: it was designed as the top chamber of a double lock and traces of the masonry for the lower chamber can be seen below the bridge at its tail. Below the lock the canal is still in the country; we noticed that this level was being dredged from the bank by a mechanical excavator. 11th, 10th and 9th Locks come close together, with their lock-keeper living by 10th Lock. 9th Lock is a double lock beside the industrial village of **Clondalkin**.

Below 9th Lock I noted the first bicycles and the first tip of rubbish in the canal: the predecessors of many. Before 8th Lock, on the north side, are the filter beds through which water which has run down from the summit level is extracted to brew Guinness. From 8th Lock down to 1st Lock the locks come thick and fast: the lock-keeper for 8th and 7th Locks lives at the 7th, for 6th and 5th at the 5th, for 4th and 3rd at the 4th, and for 2nd and 1st at 1st. 3rd Lock and 1st Lock are double locks.

This is the back door to **Dublin**—an industrial wilderness. The canal passes blocks of bleak flats and the backs of factories which ignore it to face the road, interspersed with patches of waste ground inhabited by tinkers. The weather was hot while I was there, and the locks had become populous swimming pools, the occupants of which rather resented our lowering the level by several feet.

Below 1st Lock the Circular Line branches off to the right. Ahead stretches the canal to **James's St Harbour**, but what was once a busy waterway is now a weed choked, debris strewn backwater. Much of the harbour has been filled in and when the CIE maintenance depot has moved to Tullamore this section will probably be closed.

CIRCULAR LINE, FIRST LOCK TO RINGSEND

(See strip map 6, p 136.)

Once on the Circular Line the worst is over, although we found another navigational hazard in the form of submerged—and so invisible—towpaths beneath the bridges. The branch follows a roughly semicircular course of 3¾ miles through the city to Ringsend docks. The first couple of miles to **Portobello** are level. Here was the starting point for passenger boats, but the harbour has been filled in and the former hotel is a nursing home. There follow 7 locks, at intervals of about ¼ mile, to Ringsend. The lock-keeper for the locks at Portobello, Charlemont Street, Leeson Street and Baggot Street (down boats only) lives at 47 Lennox Street (near Portobello). The lock-keeper for the locks at Baggot Street (up boats only), Upper Mount Street and Lower Mount Street, and Maquay Lock, lives at 53 Percy Place, by Upper Mount Street Lock. Wide footboards have recently been installed at these locks.

This section is most attractive. In other cities canals are shunned, hidden in deep cuttings or behind high walls; but Dublin's canal is laid out as an integral part of the Georgian city. It is an adornment to it, lined by lawns and trees, faced by eighteenth-century terraces neat with their restrained elegance. The comparison is Amsterdam, not Birmingham.

By Baggot Street Lock a seat commemorates a poet, Patrick Kavanagh, in the way that he wished. (He was, apparently, something of a local character.) Huband Bridge, at the tail of Upper Mount Street Lock, was ornamented at his own expense by the Grand Canal Company director whose name it bears. Our passage, on a fine summer evening, attracted some attention: by Lower Mount Street Lock I estimated there were over 100 onlookers.

The size of **Ringsend** basin, which you enter under a long, low, railway bridge like a rat out of a drain, is a revelation. It is enormous. And it is only the inner basin; beyond a lifting bridge (adequate headroom for most cruisers when lowered) is the outer basin, larger still. By building these basins, the canal company hoped to attract coastal shipping. Today they are almost deserted—there were two barges and a rowing boat in the outer basin. Beyond the tide locks, which have a resident lock-keeper, ships can be seen in the Liffey.

BARROW LINE, LOWTOWN TO ATHY

(See strip maps 7–8, p 137.)

The Barrow Line of the Grand Canal leaves the main line at **Lowtown**, below 19th Lock. It did not always do so: originally, boats used the first 1½ miles of what is now the Milltown Feeder. This can be seen from the newer canal, parallel and at a higher level, as can the remains of the former 19th Lock, Barrow Line, where the newer canal joins the old above Ballyteigue bridge. The water in this part of the Barrow Line is crystal clear (fish watchers enjoy looking over the bows).

The 20th and 21st Locks, Barrow Line, come close together, with the lock-keeper living at 20th. There follows a long stretch of bog, above which the canal is carried by an embankment. Part of the bog has been planted as forest. The view to the east is dominated by the Hill of Allen, crowned by a round tower which is in fact a Victorian folly. The lock-keeper for 22nd and 23rd Locks lives at 22nd Lock.

Rathangan has old warehouses and quays before its bridge, but the best mooring is a quay on the west bank just beyond the bridge. The main part of this quiet country town is to the west of the canal. The 23rd Lock is a little beyond the town.

The canal continues through a countryside of prosperous farms which is pleasant without being outstanding. The fertility of the land here seems to extend to the canal, which becomes much overgrown by reeds and weed; but always I found a clear passageway, one boat's width, to lead onwards. The 24th Lock is another double lock, with resident lock-keeper. The canal passes under the main line railway again and enters **Monasterevin** (pronounced Monster-evin).

There is a quay on the east bank, with the centre of the town a few minutes' walk down the street that leads from it, and deserted warehouses opposite. The canal then turns sharply to the right, a blind corner around which Monasterevin drawbridge appears. This is a graceful, white painted structure, which carried a link road and has a spindly appearance that belies the effort needed to raise it. There is work for two people, and the lock-keeper from 25th Lock, $\frac{1}{4}$ mile down the towpath, is in charge. Mooring posts are provided on either side of it, and there are gates to close across the road while it is raised. Operators check a safety ratchet hidden under a wooden cover and then raise the bridge with a lock key.

Monasterevin aqueduct over the River Barrow follows immediately. At the end of the aqueduct, the closed Mountmellick branch diverges to the right and the Barrow Line turns to the left. A little beyond is 25th Lock, with the lock-keeper living beside it. At the tail of the lock the canal bends to the right to regain the same alignment that it had at the approach to Monasterevin: and in fact before the aqueduct was built the canal was straight here, descending into the river and ascending out of it again by flights of locks. The remains of a bridge on this course can be seen down the road from the drawbridge.

Below 25th Lock is a level of 13 miles, the second longest on the canal. Shortly after the lock, at Clogheen Bridge, a modern structure, the canal passes under the T5, the main road from Dublin to Limerick. There are two smaller aqueducts on this level, over tributaries of the Barrow, and between them, at the small village of **Vicarstown**, a quay and more warehouses. The 26th Lock is the first of three by which the canal descends through the town of **Athy** (population 3,800, early closing Thursday) to the River Barrow. The lock-keeper for 26th and 27th Locks lives at the 27th; extensive quays above this lock, and mills and warehouses along the banks, testify to a former abundance of traffic. The 28th Lock has a resident lock-keeper; at its tail, the canal joins the River Barrow Navigation.

CHAPTER FOUR

The River Barrow Navigation[1]

The River Barrow Navigation I found to be lovely but deserted. So few boats pass that even the swans fail to associate them with food: they paddle by, instead of gathering for gifts of bread. From its start at Athy down as far as Carlow the navigation resembles an unfrequented Thames, with the addition of intricate little side canals, rich with weed and tree trunks, that lead to the locks. Below Carlow there are silted, weed-grown lock cuts and dilapidated locks, interspersed with stretches of river which are choked with weeds, or fast flowing and rocky, or—sheer delight—broad and apparently deep. By contrast with the navigation itself, the region through which it passes is prosperous, one of the most fertile in Ireland. Bustling country towns and villages, although by no means cruising oriented, make it easy to get supplies. For its final 10 miles to St Mullins Tide Lock the navigation runs through narrow valleys overlaid with steep woods; and if the usual comparison with the Rhine is more optimistic than accurate, it is certainly still delightful.

From Athy to St Mullins is 41½ miles with 23 locks, including the tide lock. The navigation works were built between 1759 and 1790. In 1894 the Barrow Navigation Co was purchased by the Grand Canal Co and the Barrow became part of the Grand Canal system. The navigation authority is CIE Canal Section (Civil Engineering Department, Pearse Station, Westland Row, Dublin 2), and regulations about

[1] See pages 138 to 140 for River Barrow Navigation strip maps.

size of craft, etc, are as detailed in the previous chapter except that maximum draught is reduced to 2ft 6in in dry summers. Lock permits, at the usual charge of 2s 3d a lock, are obtainable from the address above, from the canal depot, Tullamore, and from lock-keepers at Carlow, Graiguenamanagh and Shannon Harbour.

The River Barrow Navigation has been adversely affected by an arterial drainage scheme carried out in the upper catchment area of the river in the early thirties. Water is able to run off the land quickly, which causes sudden floods in the river after heavy rain. For example, in four days from 31 October to 3 November 1968, the level of water over the deep sill of Carlow Lock rose from 6ft 6in to 11ft 2in. During dry periods there is insufficient reserve of water at the head of the river to maintain the depth of the navigation. And silt carried down by the floods is deposited in the still waters of lock cuts and locks.

The condition of the navigation works at the time of my cruise in August 1969 left something to be desired. The chamber of Upper Ballyellan Lock, for instance, was so silted that, with the lock empty, there were only some 9 to 10in of water and I was obliged to tilt my outboard to enter. Silt or obstructions prevented any of the gates from being opened fully, and the cut below the lock was badly silted. There were similarly shallow cuts below Bagenalstown, Feniscourt, Slyguff and Clashganny Locks, and many of the cuts above locks were overgrown with weed—at Slyguff for instance there was a channel perhaps 2ft wide between masses of floating vegetation. There was a balance beam missing from one of the gates at Rathellan Lock and one broken at Ballinagrane Lock.

CIE states that during the past twenty years dredging has been carried out on an average of twenty-two weeks each year and that, since my cruise, most of the lock gates have been overhauled and dredging has been carried out at Upper Ballyellan and Clashganny Locks and below Carlow.

I probably saw the river at its worst—it was the end of a

long dry summer, water was down, and weed growth very definitely up—the worst for years, I was told. There were sections of river choked from bank to bank with feathery weed. Going downstream through them I wearied of clearing the propeller every few yards and found it easier to cut the engine and drift. Coming upstream there was fortunately less tendency for the weed to entangle itself with the propeller. The Barrow has the reputation of being a spring and autumn river, for at these seasons there should be sufficient depth of water without too many floods and too much weed.

I navigated a four-berth hire cruiser, from the Shannon, from Athy to Carlow and back in June 1969 without difficulty, except for an old anorak which wrapped itself suddenly and solidly around the propeller and sent us out of control through Carlow bridge. From Carlow to St Mullins and back I used a 16ft 4in Micro-plus cruiser with 18hp outboard: and this combination, though ludicrously overpowered for English inland waterways, I found just about right for the Barrow. Cruising a little under full throttle gave about 18mph; against wind and current, I judged this reduced in places to a land speed of only 4 or 5mph. Boats for the Barrow should be high powered and have easily accessible propellers. 'Weedless' propellers would be helpful.

There is a slipway, of a sort, at Carlow, though even its proprietor, Mr Shirley of Barrow Line Holiday Cruisers Ltd, Dublin Road, Carlow, would agree that it has room for improvement. He has plans to concrete it. It is available to visitors by arrangement at their risk.

The clue to navigating the Barrow is to bear in mind that it was made navigable for horse-drawn barges, and the navigation channel was therefore dredged some 25ft out from the towpath. It generally remains there today, although horse-drawn barges have long since gone and the towpath is often quite overgrown. (CIE tells me that extra gangs have been employed to cut bushes and overgrowth.) There are a few exceptions to the course of the navigation channel—principally where tributaries, entering on the towpath side, have made shoals, and at bridges where some arch more central and convenient than that adjacent to the towpath bank has come to be used. At the instigation of local members of the IWAI navigation arches of bridges are now marked in the same way as those on the Shannon, with a patch of red paint to port and black paint to starboard, going upstream. Local IWAI members are also obtaining a weed-cutter.

In some places the river is wide and appears clear all the way across. In others it is definitely not clear and away from the dredged channel large rocks and boulders appear above the surface. The towpath bank is often soft enough for boats to approach, with caution, and moor. I found polaroid spectacles valuable for spotting shallows, rocks and weed below the surface. Most lock cuts commence at a weir, open, often difficult to spot from upstream, and frequently of L-shaped plan so that it is necessary to cruise parallel to part of the weir before entering the cut. These cuts range in length from a few yards to a couple of miles; below locks, cuts are mostly short, and the deep gates of locks can usually be spotted from the river by boats coming upstream. Locks are operated in the same way as those on the Grand Canal.

The Barrow Navigation appears on Ordnance Survey half-inch scale maps sheets 16 and 19, and on one-inch scale maps sheets 128, 137, 147 and 157.

Going downstream, boats enter the River Barrow Navigation at **Athy**, at the tail of 28th Lock, Grand Canal Barrow Line. Here is a good example of the 'follow the course of a horse-drawn barge' precept. The lock is on the west bank of the river; the towpath, to port as you leave the lock, is carried over to the east bank of the river by a long narrow stone bridge called the Horse Bridge (under which the navigation does not go). So the channel goes straight across the river before turning south. Immediately downstream is an L-shaped weir and the entrance to the Ardreigh lock cut next the east bank. Built over the cross-river part of the weir is a concrete railway bridge, not shown on the half-inch map. Its easternmost arch spans the lock cut; the remainder are over the weir. Towpath and lock cuts continue on the east bank as far as Carlow.

There is a lifting bridge shortly before Ardreigh Lock, which is usually, though not invariably, left up. The lock-keeper for 28th, Ardreigh and Levitstown Locks lives at 28th Lock. About a mile below the lock is a weir and the entrance to Levitstown lock cut. This is 2 miles long, the longest on the navigation. There is another lifting bridge, again shortly before the lock. Its deck lifts vertically when a handle is wound, after the safety catch has been set. The cut enters the river below the lock: a large castellated ruin between lock and river is a useful landmark when coming upstream.

The channel, following the towpath, passes to the east of an island above Maganey bridge, which can be seen from the distance. There is a quay on the east bank. The second arch of the bridge from the east bank is marked for navigation. A little further on is a small island close to the east bank: here the navigation course passes outside it. Maganey weir, cut and lock follow: coming upstream, the lock cottage can be seen before the entrance to the cut. The lock-keeper for Maganey, Bestfield and Carlow Locks lives at Carlow Lock. A $\frac{1}{4}$ mile below Maganey Lock the Greese River enters under a bridge beneath the towpath—it has made a shoal at its mouth. Bestfield weir, cut and lock I found straightforward.

At **Carlow** (population 7,700, early closing Thursday), the arch of the bridge nearest to the east bank is marked for navigation. It appears suddenly round a corner and the third arch from the east bank is also used. Below the bridge the navigation channel cuts across to the west bank above the weir to the lock, gay with flowers. Channel, towpath, lock cuts and locks are now on the west side of the river until just below the bridge at Leighlinbridge. There are quays at Carlow on the east bank below the bridge and the west bank above the lock. The main part of the town is on the east bank.

Page 85 Lough Corrib Navigation: (*above*) the waterbus leaves Annaghdown quay. In the distance are the remains of the Norman castle; (*below*) farthest west—Maam Bridge, Connemara, looking upstream. The best mooring is to the far bank, beyond the boat

Page 86 The Erne: (*above*) broad lough: looking out on to part of Lower Lough Erne from Lustybeg Island; (*below*) winding river: craft and crews gather at the Killyhevlin Hotel quay for the IWAI end of season mini-rally

Below the mouth of the lock cut boats should cruise down the centre of the river for about 100yd to avoid a shoal before coming over to the west bank. The entrance to Clogrennan lock cut is about a mile below Carlow Lock—there is no weir in sight and it is indicated by a post on the bank bearing a white arrow pointing down the cut. The cut is long and secluded, lined with woods.

The lock-keeper for Clogrennan, Milford and Rathvindon Locks lives near Milford Lock. Below Clogrennan Lock the channel re-enters the river immediately. The west side of the river is again shoal for a few hundred yards. The entrance to Milford lock cut is spanned by a canal-type bridge; further down the cut is a lifting bridge worked by pulling down a chain. The lock-keeper lives at a cottage up the road on the west bank from this bridge. Below the lock is a fast flowing section of river; the channel passes to the west of two islands. Rathvindon weir I found so obscured by reeds that I had spotted the adjacent cut entrance before noticing the weir. The lock presented no difficulty and the cut again rejoins the river immediately below.

Upstream of **Leighlinbridge** (pronounced Locklinbridge) the channel passes west of an island and there is a quay on the west bank before the bridge. The navigation arch is marked and immediately below the bridge the navigation channel crosses to the east bank. Leighlinbridge bridge, built in 1320, is probably the oldest on the river.

The navigation channel, towpath, lock cuts and locks are now on the east side of the river for the rest of the way to St Mullins. Half a mile below Leighlinbridge is a weir and the entrance to a mile long cut leading to Rathellan Lock. Above the lock on the east side are the remains of a dry dock and workshops. The lock-keeper for Rathellan, Bagenalstown and Fenniscourt Locks lives at Fenniscourt Lock.

Below the lock the navigation re-enters the river for ½ mile until another weir and the start of the long, still, deep quay-lined cut past **Bagenalstown**. In writing, this place is sometimes given its Irish name of Muine Bheag, but in conversation it always seems to be Bagenalstown. The town with most facilities is set back from the east bank.

From Bagenalstown to Borris I found the most adventurous part of the Barrow, with the shallowest and fastest flowing river sections, the most weedy and silted side canals, and, with one exception, the locks in worst condition. The lifting bridge at the entrance to Bagenalstown Lock is a good start: it is heavy enough to need at least two people pulling down on the chains to raise it. Bagenalstown Lock is deep and the upper sill is a series of steps which might catch an unwary descending boat. At the opposite end of the lock, on the east side, is an outfall of water from the adjacent mill, just below the surface when the lock is full.

Below Royal Oak bridge is an island and although the channel passes to the east of this I found it badly shoaled. From a distance the navigation arch of the railway viaduct appeared obstructed by reeds. Fenniscourt Lock, by contrast with most, is well kept and surrounded by gardens of near Thames Conservancy smartness. Here, going downstream, I passed the first boat seen since leaving Carlow.

Slyguff lock cut starts by the weir just over a mile downstream. The lock-keeper for Slyguff, Upper and Lower Ballyellan and Ballytiglea Locks comes from Graiguenamanagh and is, according to CIE, in attendance during the day. The entrance to the cut below Slyguff Lock is difficult to spot when coming up river as the lock is out of sight. The worst of the weed in the river was, I found, between Slyguff and Upper Ballyellan Locks, right across the river for several hundred yards. There was much feathery weed also at the entrance to Upper Ballyellan lock cut, where the channel runs alongside the head of the weir.

At **Goresbridge** the second arch of the bridge from the east bank is marked for navigation, but I found it weeded up and, following local advice, used the arch next the towpath which was satisfactory. There is a quay on the east bank below the bridge; the village is the other side of the river. The weir and entrance to Lower Ballyellan lock cut are $\frac{1}{2}$ mile downstream. The next reach from Lower Ballyellan Lock to Ballytiglea Lock is fast flowing, and reedy and rocky away from the channel. Until Ballytiglea the scenery has been merely pleasant, but here the hills close in on either side and the river starts to run through its defile to the sea. Below Ballytiglea Lock the current continued strong; I could see boulders below the boat through the clear water, while others broke the surface away to the west side of the river. Viewing this rocky, rushy torrent from the heights of Ballytiglea bridge it was difficult to believe it a navigation at all. The second arch of the bridge from the east bank is marked for navigation.

Borris and Ballinagrane Locks are marked on the half-inch map but not on the one-inch. The lock-keeper for these two, and for Clashganny and Ballykeenan Locks, lives at Clashganny Lock. Below Borris Lock the river becomes wide and weed-free; the river sections of the navigation continued like this to St Mullins Tide Lock. Lush meadows and orchards against a backdrop of steep conifer-covered hills gave Clashganny Lock a Tyrolean air. There follows a short section of river where the bed, seen through clear water, consists of large, solid, rocks which looked uncomfortably close to the surface. Some of these were probably positioned intentionally, a couple of hundred years ago, to prevent erosion of the towpath. The entrance to the long cut leading to Ballykeenan Lock appears suddenly round a corner; there is no weir visible.

Ballykeenan is a double lock, with not much fall in the upper chamber and a footbridge over the lower. A reach of wide river leads between the hillsides to **Graiguenamanagh** (early closing Wednesday). A $\frac{1}{4}$ mile or so of deserted quays, above the bridge on the west bank and below it on the east, suggest that Graigue (to which the full name is habitually contracted, with the 'ue' silent) was once a busy inland port. Today it is a good goal for a cruising holiday—a charming place set on a bend of the river and overlooked by the high hump of Brandon Hill. The Barrow, in my opinion, could well do with a boat rally on the lines of the Shannon Rally; if, as I am told, owners of boats on the Shannon are reluctant to leave that waterway, they are missing something good.

The second arch of Graigue bridge from the east bank is marked for navigation and below it is the weir and Graigue Lock. The lock-keeper for Graigue, Lower Tinnahinch, Carriglead and St Mullins Locks lives here. The $\frac{1}{2}$ mile long canal to Lower Tinnahinch Lock was shallow, weedy and fast flowing. Three-quarters of a mile further downstream are Carriglead weir and lock.

In the reach of broad river which follows are several scars or ledges of rock which stretch across the river from the west bank, showing above water level, and were presumably cut through to make the navigation. At another point a large dead tree lay in the river close to the east bank but it was safe, I was told, to pass outside this. About $1\frac{1}{2}$ miles below Carriglead Lock is a weir and the entrance to the $\frac{1}{2}$ mile canal which leads to St Mullins Lock. And there, at a remote and beautiful spot, the hills are at their highest, but the navigation, perversely, has reached sea level.

CHAPTER FIVE

The Lough Corrib Navigation

Corrib runs from Galway up into the hills of Connemara. This region is well on the tourist track; it has superb scenery, fine fishing, Connemara ponies and plenty of other attractions. Despite these (or perhaps because of them), Corrib's potential for cruising is almost entirely neglected. This is a pity. The scenery is superior to any of the Shannon lakes, and Corrib is too big to see adequately from one base by day boat. It offers ample scope for a cruising holiday of a week, or a leisurely fortnight; and trailable-cruiser owners should put it high on their visiting list.

Custom divides Lough Corrib into Lower and Upper Lakes. The Lower Lake, near to Galway, is shallow, often rocky, and surrounded by the flat country of the limestone plain; but the Upper Lake, beyond Rabbit Island, is deep and wide. In both parts of the lough are many islands—allegedly, of course, 365! As you come up from Galway, a range of hills appears dimly through the haze to the north-west, grows slowly larger, resolves itself into the mountains of the Joyce Country and finally closes in on fiords which lead to Maam with some of the finest scenery on any inland waterway in Ireland.

From Galway to Corrib's furthest extremity at Maam Bridge is 27 miles as the crow flies, nearer 40 miles by the navigation channel. The greatest width of the lake is 10 miles, and its area is 68 sq miles.

Corrib was made navigable in the 1850s for steamers. The

navigation authority is the Lough Corrib Navigation Trustees, 22 Lr Dominick Street, Galway. It maintains the navigation channel, marks and beacons, piers and quays in good order. It is financed by the ratepayers of Galway and Mayo; there are no licensing or other charges for boats, no mooring fees, and use of public piers and quays is free.

Corrib is now isolated from the sea. Formerly it was possible to enter it through the Eglinton Canal at Galway. This connection was destroyed in 1954 when its swing bridges were replaced by low-level fixed bridges. Its two fine large locks remain, in near perfect order, and with a bridge on either side of one of them so low that a rowing boat has difficulty in passing beneath. There are no other bridges on the Lough Corrib Navigation.

There are neither hire cruisers nor commercial craft on Corrib. The nearest approach to the latter are about 500 fishing boats, with oars and, usually, outboard engines, and the *Maid of Coleraine*, a fine modern waterbus formerly on the River Bann which now operates out of Galway. There are a dozen or so privately owned cruisers.

A hindrance to the introduction of hire cruisers on Corrib is the shortage of suitable sheltered quays. The trustees' quays (and the trustees can only maintain what they are entrusted with) are large, designed for lake steamers and often exposed. Smaller harbours on the lake shores are intended for shallow draught fishing boats. The usual four or five berth hire cruiser would be too small to lie comfortably at the former in bad weather, but too large to enter the latter. This disadvantage does not apply to small trailer-borne cruisers, which can often enter the small harbours, at any rate with outboard tilted. There is plenty of scope for sailing in the main part of the Upper Lake, but in the approaches to Maam the proximity of mountains makes winds very variable.

The prevailing wind is west or south-west, but a north-east wind gives best conditions. Bad conditions produce a swell in the deep water off Cong 'as big as the waves in Galway Bay', and poor visibility sometimes makes it difficult to see the markers. Personally, I enjoyed clear sunny weather throughout my stay on the lake, but I have seen a south wind reduce the water level at Galway by about 9in.

Facilities such as waterside fuel supplies are absent. I indicate below a few petrol stations near the lake. To obtain drinking water is something of a test of initiative. Locals say they drink lake water without ill-effect.

The Admiralty chart for Lough Corrib is no 5079. Drainage schemes have reduced the level by about 1ft and silted some of the channels. Corrib appears on Ordnance Survey one-inch map sheets 94, 95 and 105 and half-inch sheets 11 and 14.

Markers indicate the navigation courses from Galway to Cong, Oughterard and Maam. There are 153 of them, mostly perches and stone beacons (the latter locally called monuments), with a few buoys near Galway. I found them freshly painted and not generally difficult to spot. But the code of marking is unusual. It is immediately necessary to forget anything you may have learnt elsewhere about leaving red to port and black to starboard when going upstream. On Corrib, going from Galway to Cong, Oughterard or Maam, you leave to starboard any marker that is red, or red and white, or white; and to port any marker that is black or black and yellow. Topmarks, when fitted to starboard markers, are circular or oval grids, and, when fitted to port markers, diamond shaped grids. Most of the markers are in the narrow part of the lake, and at the approaches to Cong and Oughterard. The rest of the Upper Lake is generally deep except near shore and islands. Shores are usually rocky, but the water I found clear enough to be able to spot obstructions.

Galway (population about 22,000, early closing day Thursday) is, after Dublin, the largest city on an Irish inland waterway. It should be able to provide most needs of visiting boaters. Shops are good, and some are splendidly old-

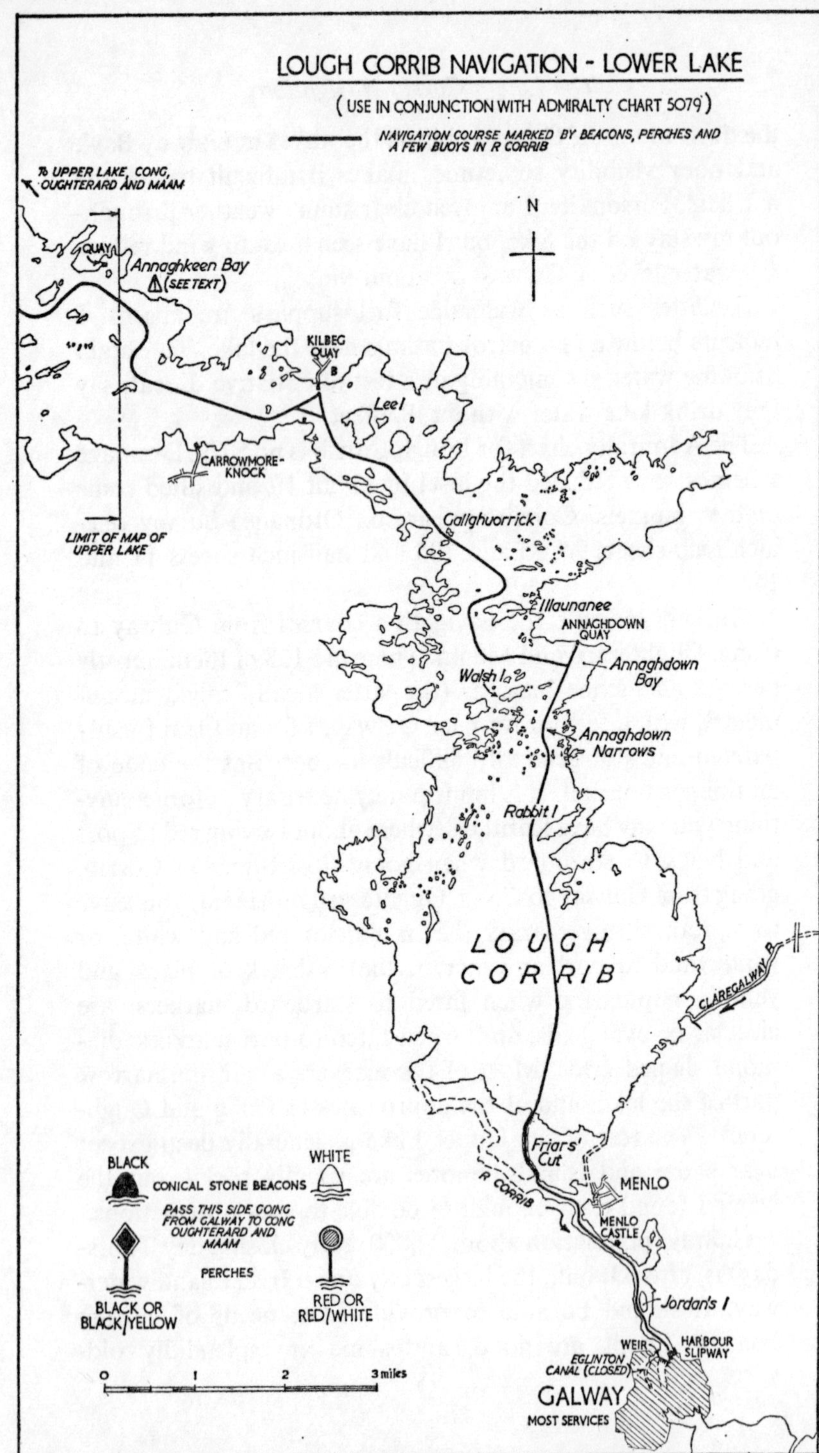

Based on the Ordnance Survey by permission of the Government (Permit No 1427)

fashioned. The lake harbour and a good slipway are at Woodquay, on the north side of the town and the east bank of the River Corrib. They can be approached from Headford Road without passing through the centre of the city; there are several petrol stations along this road.

The navigation channel in the river follows the centre except where markers indicate otherwise, and passes west of Jordans Island. The quay at Menlo, visible on the east bank, I found to be badly silted. Electricity cables cross the river in several places. The Friars' Cut, the short artificial cut from the river to the Lower Lake built, probably, in the twelfth century by Franciscan friars, was widened in 1846 for steamers and again in 1954 for drainage.

The entrance to the Lower Lake is silted and a narrow channel of about 3ft 6in depth passes between pairs of red-and-white and black-and-white posts. Coming south, a pyramidal white hoarding indicates the entrance to the cut from a distance, and from still further away locals steer the correct course by aiming for a hill on the horizon with two humps like a camel's. This part of the Lower Lake I found wide, rather bleak, full of waterfowl. I navigated the Claregalway River for 1½ miles to within sight of the main road bridge and found it deep and weed free (unlike its approaches in the lake) and with soft banks for mooring. It passes between farmland and bog. White beacons lead the main course north to the Annaghdown Narrows. Beacons are visible from a far greater distance than perches. I had to keep a sharp look-out, when steering towards distant beacons, for perches which required a deviation from the direct course.

Either side of the narrows, many rocky shoals show above water. The channel, well marked, twists and turns between them. When it enters Annaghdown Bay, **Annaghdown** quay is straight ahead. I found deep water off the end of it, where the water bus moors, and a shallow harbour for lake boats alongside. Five minutes' walk up the road are the remains of Annaghdown Abbey, founded by St Brendan the Navigator.

I was told of plans for a hotel by the quay; but there are no facilities at present.

Markers lead a winding channel from Annaghdown to Kilbeg. It would be easy to miss a marker, cut a corner, and finish on the rocks. A desolate flat landscape of bare rocks and water stretches away to the distance.

Kilbeg has a deep quay on the east shore, with a pub nearby. I could find no route to the quay on the west shore, served by a ferry according to the map. Rocks in the water suggest that the black perches off it mean what they say. At **Carrowmoreknock** (according to the Ordnance Survey; but local pronunciation varies) is a shallow harbour for lake boats, with a small village up the road.

Annaghkeen bay is strewn with unmarked rocky shoals below water level. To reach the shallow quay on the west shore of the bay I left the island at the entrance of the bay to port, passed between it and a shoal marked by a stake, and steered a circuitous course around shoals which I could see through the clear water. The quay by the twelfth-century castle had fallen stonework off it.

Beyond Annaghkeen the water widens out into the Upper Lake. Away to starboard is Inchiquin island, connected to the mainland by a causeway, since the inhabitants refused to pay their rates until one was provided.

The approach to **Oughterard** is marked in the normal way, but a second row of black perches away to the west caused me some confusion. Oughterard steamer quay is deep, and rather exposed. It may be improved. The village is a mile up the road. Small craft get closer by ascending the Owenriff River, but this has a silt bar at the mouth. Even following local advice to keep 30ft to the west of a red post (which is not a navigation mark, but indicates a water intake for some cottages) I had the skeg of my outboard in the sand. The river itself is sheltered and appears deep; one or two cruisers based in it are poled across the bar. I moored to the east bank.

Oughterard (population 600) I thought a pleasant place,

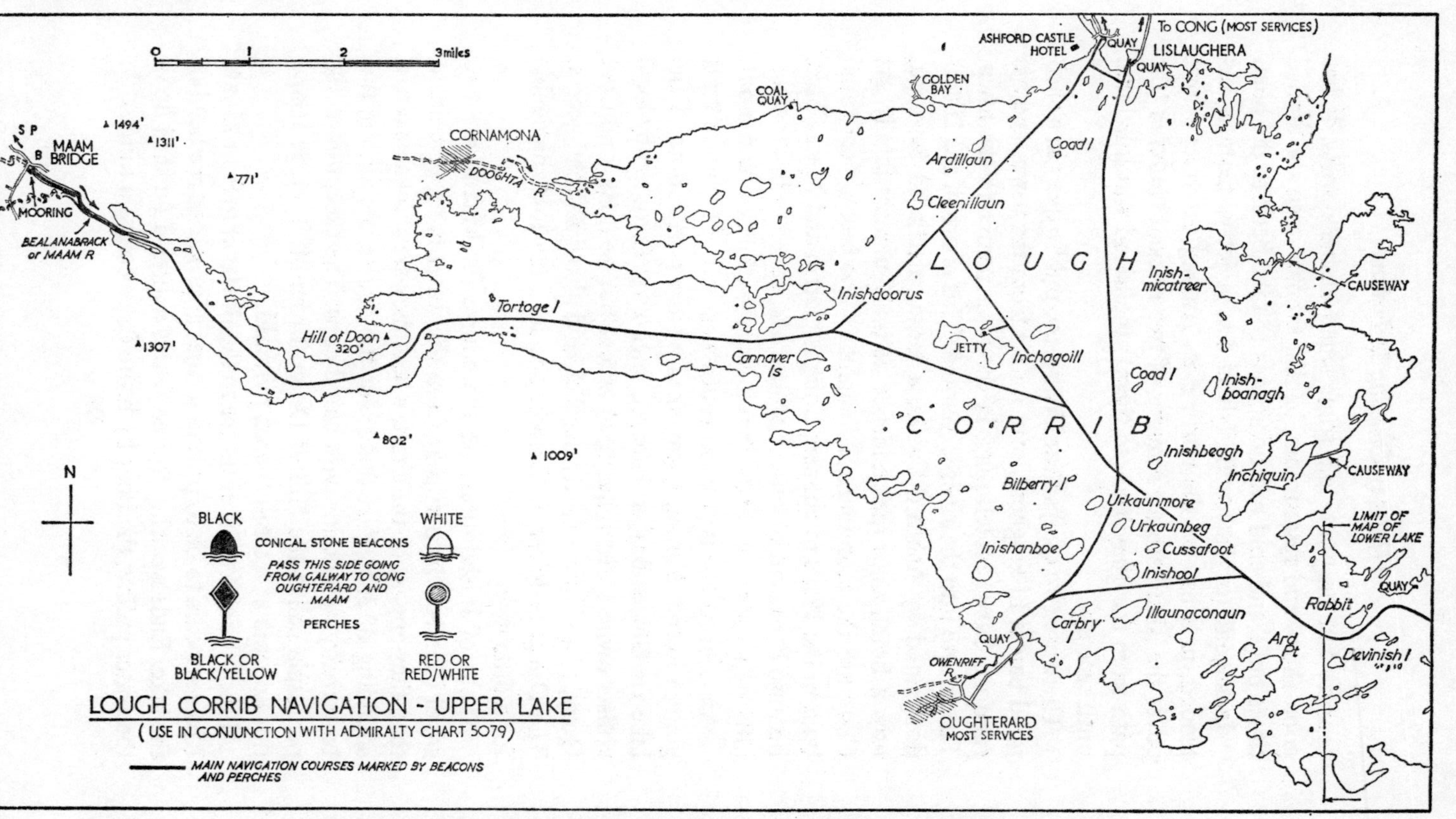

Based on the Ordnance Survey by permission of the Government (Permit No 1427)

touristy but unspoilt, like some small alpine resorts. It has good shops and restaurants, banks, though open for limited times only, and cold roast chickens to take back to the boat.

Inchagoill (or Inchagill) Island has a jetty, recently extended, in a bay on the north side. Among the trees which cover the island are the remains of two ancient churches (the path from the quay leads to them); the island was inhabited until recently.

There are two quays near **Cong**—the public quay in a sheltered bay at Lislaughera, over a mile from the town, and the Ashford Castle Hotel quay, in the river nearer to the town. The course into the river is marked. This shore of the lake is dominated by Ashford Castle, a large castellated mansion, now a hotel, once the residence of the Guinness family. At Cong are the monumental remains of the incomplete canal built in the 1850s to connect Loughs Corrib and Mask. This, because it was cut through porous rock, failed to hold water, although it seems as likely that it was the money that ran out.

Another course is marked south-west out of Cong for craft going towards Maam. Unmarked on the north shore of the lake are **Golden Bay**, a sheltered anchorage favoured by local cruiser owners which has road access but no quay, and **Coal Quay**, an old quay, partly derelict, and also with road access. The Dooghta River at Cornamona is, I am told, navigable for a little way.

South of Inishdoorus, on the course for Maam, are two small islands, which appear from the water more prominent than they appear on the chart, where they are shown next to a sounding of 30ft. Past this point the course lies among fine bare rocky mountains with cloud caps. The exception is the peninsula called the Hill of Doon. From off Tortoge Island this appears as a tree-covered pyramid.

From the chart, the entrance to the Bealanabrack or Maam River appears to be to port as a boat approaches the head of the lake. Endeavouring to follow this course, I finished up in the water pulling the boat by brute force across a sandbank.

Thc river appears to have silted so much that the entrance is now through a gap in the reeds to starboard. Immediately after entering the river, it is necessary to leave a backwater to starboard; a mile or so further on, the course does turn sharply to starboard while the Failmore River goes straight on. **Maam Bridge** appears round an S bend to starboard. I moored to the south bank, immediately below the bridge, where there was once a quay.

Across the bridge is a pub called the Maam Hotel, a pleasant little low roofed regency building, and about 400yd down the Leenane road is a shop and petrol station. Maam Bridge has the stillness of mountain places: on one side, the hills rise to nearly 1,500ft, on the other, beyond a bit of bog, to over 2,000. Perhaps a dozen cruisers a year, at the most, reach this ultima Thule of Irish waterways.

CHAPTER SIX

The Erne

The Erne includes broad lakes, winding rivers and numerous islands, large and small. It is short compared with the Shannon, but full of variety.

Downstream from Enniskillen the River Erne widens gradually into Lower Lough Erne, here studded with small humped islands. Many are covered with woods, some are inhabited—by people, or wild goats. The islands thin out imperceptibly and a broad sheet of water stretches away to the distance. The south shore of the wide part of the lake is overshadowed by a craggy escarpment, called the Poola Fooka range by the Admiralty chart, which rises more than 900ft above it. At the far end of the lake the river leads to Belleek.

Above Enniskillen, which is itself on an island, broad channels with little current meander through a charming countryside, reaching round and encircling little hills here and there. The islands so formed are scarcely to be appreciated as such—they are 1, 2 or 3 miles across with bridges to the mainland. Beyond is Upper Lough Erne, again with many small islands, not unlike the nearer part of the Lower Lough. But the water does not open out further, rather the shores close in to make a labyrinth of remote bays and secretive reedy lagoons. Through them the Border between Northern Ireland and the Irish Republic winds its own inconsequential way, conspicuous on the map and invisible on the water. Beyond again is river, reaching down to Belturbet in the republic.

It is around 55 miles by the shortest waterborne route from Belleek to Belturbet. The broad part of Lower Lough Erne is 9 miles long by 5 miles across at the widest: it is the more northerly of the two loughs. Most of the navigable Erne is in Northern Ireland, in County Fermanagh which is said to be one-third water. But such are the contortions of the Border that it impinges on the waterway not only near Belturbet at its southern end but also, briefly, at the opposite end at Belleek. Geologically, much of the area is glacial in origin, and the small humped hills and islands are drumlins. Mary Rogers, in her compact and encyclopaedic study of the region, *Prospect of Erne*, reduces the traditional 365 islands to an actual 154, that is 57 in the upper lake and 97 in the lower.

The Erne has few waterside villages. Because of its former tendency to flood, villages were built away from the water on higher ground. Many of the public quays were previously ferry slipways. By way of compensation, there are two good country house hotels close to the water—the Killyhevlin which has its own pier a couple of miles above Enniskillen, and the Manor House which overlooks Killadeas quay. Both welcome boating people.

Upper Lough Erne, and the lower lake as far as Owl Island, are probably the best waters in Ireland for beginners to cruising. Shores are mostly soft mud or shingle, and rocks are few. (There are plenty further down the lower lake.) Shelter is never far away. The navigation markers are the clearest on any Irish waterway. Yet there is no statutory navigation authority.

Most of the markers at present in use were installed after a drainage and hydro-electric scheme in the fifties. (The power station is below Belleek.) In Northern Ireland, they are maintained by the Drainage Division of the Ministry of Agriculture (York Buildings, 2 Curtis Street, Belfast BT1 2PF). Additional markers are being installed at the instigation of the Fermanagh County Council. Markers in the republic, in the river up to Belturbet, are maintained as a praiseworthy voluntary effort by the local branch of the IWAI. All work on the same system, and comprise a perch with a top mark painted with red lead.

Going towards Belturbet, markers to be left to port have semicircular top marks with horizontal diameters uppermost. Those to be left to starboard have similar top marks the other way up—with the round part uppermost. '*L*evel top *l*eft, *r*ound top *r*ight' is the mnemonic; alternatively, leave the markers shaped like port wine glasses to port. But these mental gymnastics are now mostly unnecessary, for green strips have been painted on the top marks, down the edge by which it is safe to pass them. Indeed some markers recently installed in minor channels have small circular top marks, their safe side indicated only by the green strip. This seems regrettable: bad light or weathered paint make distinctive shapes helpful.

There are also middle ground markers, with red diamond shaped top marks. They are used either individually, to indicate isolated shoals which can be passed either side—50yd or so from the marker—or to 'fill in' extensive shoals with limits shown by port and starboard markers. Each marker in Fermanagh has a reference number painted on it—for example, 54 B. '54' indicates a position between the 54 and 55 horizontal grid lines on the Ordnance Survey map, and is painted on all markers in this band. These markers are then lettered alphabetically from west to east. 54 B is in fact off Goat Island. The Erne is shown on one-inch Ordnance Survey of Northern Ireland map sheets 4 and 7.

In addition to markers, direction signs have been erected in the confusing region south of Enniskillen, where strangers had been known to go round in circles. The water in the Erne I found too cloudy to see rocks or shoals.

The levels of the Lower and Upper Loughs are maintained at minima of 147ft and 150ft above ordnance datum respectively. In practice they are usually at the same level and even a reverse flow of water is known past Enniskillen. When the

Page 103 (*above*) Lower Bann Navigation: Kilrea bridge, looking upstream. The navigation channel passes under the swing span at the left—a fishing boat motionless beneath it emphasises the lack of traffic. There is a small quay just before the bridge; (*below*) River Blackwater. Looking downstream from Moy bridge, with moorings on the left. The Ulster Canal once started beyond the buildings in the distance

Page 104 Navigation aids and hindrances: (*above*) Lough Neagh, a gale makes things interesting at the mouth of the Six Mile Water. The channel from the river passes between the two distant markers. The finger post in the foreground is a standard Lower Bann Navigation marker—the channel passes the side it points; (*below left*) a typical navigation marker on the Lough Corrib Navigation. Perch with black diamond topmark, to be left to *port* when going from Galway to Cong, Oughterard or Maam. The upright of this one is painted yellow as an experiment to aid visibility; (*below right*) Shannon Navigation, beacon with rectangular blank topmark, to be left to *starboard* when going upstream or entering bays and harbours

upper lake approaches its statutory minimum, as for instance at the end of a dry summer such as 1969, navigation in the upper reaches towards Belturbet and Wattle Bridge becomes difficult with shoals in the channel. The lakes flood in winter, and exceptionally as late as July, but the normal summer level corresponds fairly closely to the soundings shown on the Admiralty charts (no 5082 for Lower Lough Erne and no 5083 for Upper Lough Erne). If anything there are usually a few more inches of water in the main channel than is shown, and fords have been dredged out. A map of Lough Erne is published by G. Dibb Ltd.

The barrage at Portora, $\frac{3}{4}$ mile below Enniskillen, controls the level of the Upper Lough, but it is usually necessary to close the sluice gates only in winter. The dry summers of 1968 and 1969 have been exceptions—the sluice gates have been closed and the navigation lock alongside brought into use. When this happens a lock-keeper is on duty from 8 am to midnight. The navigation channel is through the lock at all times—when there is no difference in water level either side, all the lock gates are left open. The lock is 20ft wide and 100ft long.

There are no licensing charges for craft on the Erne, and mooring at public quays, maintained by Fermanagh County Council, is free. There are slipways at Belturbet, Round O Quay (Enniskillen), and Castle Archdale. In winds of force five and upwards the Lower Lough below Owl Island becomes choppy and uncomfortable, particularly when the wind is from north-west, west or south-west. When the weather is variable it has the reputation of being very variable: the wind blows up into gusts, then dies away. Overhead electric cables cross the waterway with clearance, I understand, sometimes as low as 20ft. Clearance of 35ft is recommended for new installations, but old ones have not been altered.

Improvements planned include better quays at Bellanaleck and Killadeas, and dredging of the Colebrooke River.

When cruising on the Erne it is worth remembering that

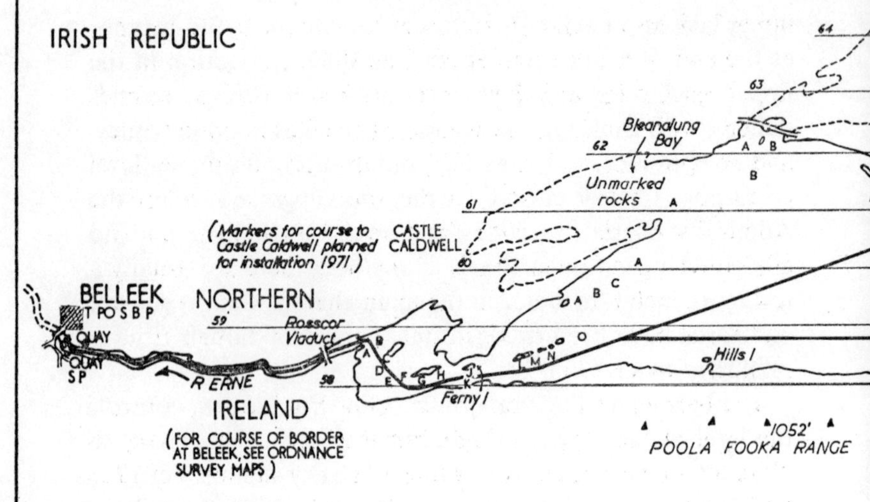

LOWER LOUGH ERNE

(USE IN CONJUNCTION WITH ADMIRALTY CHART 5082)

MAIN CRUISING COURSES

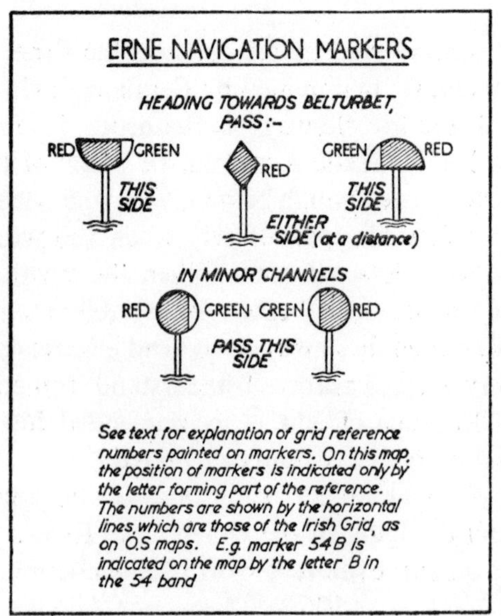

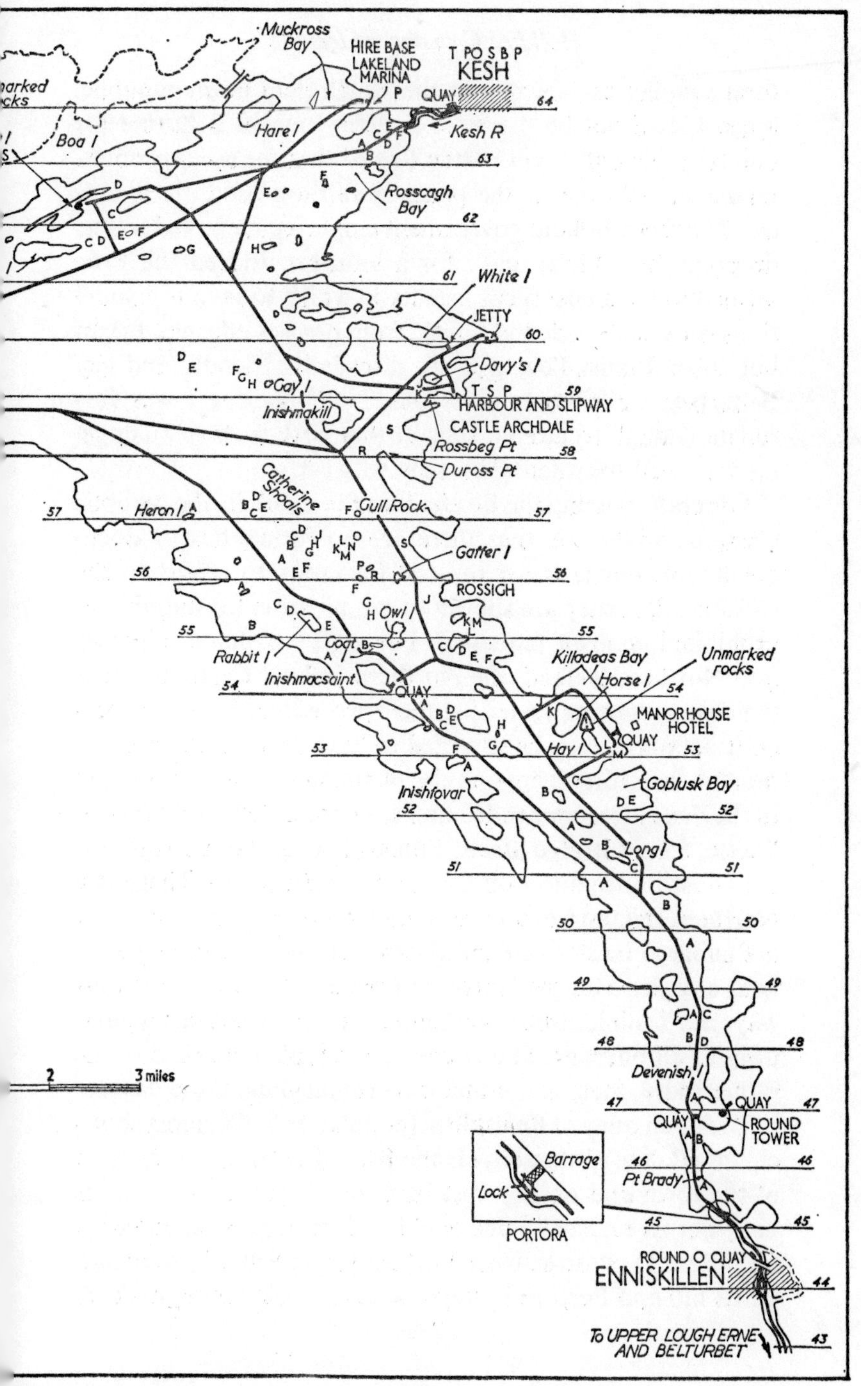

Muckross Bay
HIRE BASE LAKELAND MARINA
T PO S B P
KESH
QUAY
Kesh R
Hare I
Boa I
Rosscagh Bay
White I
JETTY
Davy's I
Gay I
Inishmakill
T S P
HARBOUR AND SLIPWAY
CASTLE ARCHDALE
Rossbeg Pt
Duross Pt
Catherine Shoals
Heron I
Gull Rock
Gaffer I
ROSSIGH
Owl I
Rabbit I
Goat I
Inishmacsaint
QUAY
Killadeas Bay
Horse I
Unmarked rocks
MANOR HOUSE HOTEL
QUAY
Hay I
Goblusk Bay
Inishfovar
Long I
Devenish I
QUAY
QUAY
ROUND TOWER
Pt Brady
Barrage
Lock
PORTORA
ROUND O QUAY
ENNISKILLEN
To UPPER LOUGH ERNE AND BELTURBET
3 miles

food supplies are cheaper in the North than in the republic. Since I shall not be the most popular man in Belturbet for pointing this out, I will hasten to add that for evening entertainment, Belturbet is the place. A rattling good place, too, as a Northern Ireland government employee remarked to me, dropping his official mask for a moment. Indeed the Erne seemed to me an excellent locality in which to savour distinctions between North and South, from precise, efficient, bright but sober Enniskillen to drab, disorderly, friendly and gay Belturbet; while boat rallies there, such as one I was fortunate enough to attend, suggest that both sorts of Irish get on very well together when they so wish.

For craft crossing the Border into the republic, the republic Customs advise me that there are no formalities or documentation, nor is there any call for crews to report to the Customs. But they are subject to examination for dutiable or prohibited goods if requested. For craft crossing the Border into Northern Ireland, the Northern Ireland Customs are at the time of writing reviewing their procedure. However, hire craft operators may be expected to have up-to-date information for their hirers; anyone else planning to launch a boat on to the Erne is recommended first to contact HM Customs and Excise, 6 East Bridge Street, Enniskillen, Co Fermanagh, for the latest information on Customs requirements. There is a Northern Ireland Customs post on Derryvore point, and craft are liable to be stopped and questioned by a Customs patrol boat anywhere on the Northern Ireland section of the waterway. But I think visitors are unlikely to find Customs regulations at all onerous; in any event, as people remarked to me rather sadly, there is nothing worth smuggling, these days.

The main quay at **Enniskillen** (population 7,200, most shops closed all day Wednesday) is the Round O Quay, to the west of the town and on the west bank of the river. The quay is new, but its unusual name is old and its origins, apparently, forgotten. Downstream are Portora Royal School prominent on its hill and Portora barrage, with the lock, through which the navigation channel passes, adjacent to the west bank. There is no channel through the arches of the barrage. Beyond is Point Brady on the east bank, also called Buttermilk Point from the frothy breakers along its shore.

Devenish Island is to the east of the navigation course. It has a jetty from which a public footpath leads over the top of the island past grazing cattle and bouncing hares to the round tower and ecclesiastical remains. There is a more sheltered jetty on the east shore of the island. A couple of miles further down the lake at Long Island the channel divides. One channel then follows the south-east and south shores and is the most direct route to Belleek. The other follows the north-east shore to most of the other harbours. They are separated by a chain of islands: the Admiralty chart shows that it is possible to pass between these from channel to channel, and also to enter many bays.

Goblusk Bay, on the north-east shore, is the headquarters of the Lough Erne Yacht Club. Beyond it is Killadeas Bay, to be entered either south of Hay Island or north of Horse Island —there are unmarked rocks between the two islands. The bay has **Killadeas** public quay with a floating jetty, and a private jetty for water skiers. The Manor House Hotel is up the hill, but there is no village near by. At **Rossigh** a promising looking jetty is deceptive—I found only a few inches of water off it. One could, no doubt, anchor in the bay and go ashore by dinghy.

Owl Island is inhabited and the bay on the east side is a sheltered anchorage from a west wind. At such times the course from here to Castle Archdale is exposed. The approach to **Castle Archdale** Harbour is between Rossbeg Point and Davy's Island; there are two old flying-boat jetties and a gently shelving slip-way to be passed to starboard before the harbour is reached. This I found to be the most sheltered on the Erne. It is part of the former flying-boat and seaplane base, now the Castle Archdale holiday centre and caravan camping park. To moor cost 7s 6d (37½p) a night, but this gave access to the centre's community building with hot and cold showers, washing and ironing room, toilets, shop, coffee bar, public telephone, two television rooms (for different channels), lounges and a games room with table tennis and such. A restaurant may be added. It sounds a good place to be on a wet day with a family boating party for whom the immediate novelty of cruising is wearing thin. The building (five minutes' walk from the harbour, up the concrete road through the trees and then half right across the caravan park) was the flying-boat base command post and the coffee bar has on the wall a stirring picture of a Sunderland flying-boat taxiing on the lake.

White Island has a jetty near its south-east corner, near the remains of an ancient church. Seven grotesque and very early Christian sculptures, found in the vicinity, have been built into the north wall—so far as I could see, in order of expression, for the face on the right has downturned mouth and downcast look, the figures in the centre show increasing degrees of contentment, and that on the left, said to be a female fertility figure of pagan origin, wears a broad grin!

On the mainland, almost opposite White Island, is a small quay in a forestry plantation. A signpost indicated that it was ¼ mile to the ruins of the first Castle Archdale.

The approach to the Kesh River in Rosscagh Bay had been marked by the time of my cruise in September 1969, but the river itself had not then been dredged. This has now been done. At **Kesh** itself is an attractive village with most facilities. In Muckross Bay nearby a hire craft operator was constructing a new harbour to be called **Lakeland Marina** and planned to have fuel and water supplies for visiting craft.

On **Lustybeg Island** ordered lawns among the trees reach back from two jetties (cruisers can reach the end of the one to starboard as they approach) to a neat whitewashed cottage guesthouse. Meals and fresh water are available to visiting cruisers, though Mr Suckling the proprietor requested that he be contacted for the latter—the pump required practised operation.

The area behind Hare and Boa (pronounced Bo) Islands is in effect unnavigable, as there is no marked channel and plenty of unmarked rocks. The same applies to Bleanalung Bay and its approaches, although there must be a channel here somewhere as steamers used to ply to Castle Caldwell. One hopes it will be marked in 1971.

The more southerly course from Long Island has fewer features. Where Lt Wolfe the Admiralty surveyor laconically remarks 'Cormorants' on his 1836 chart are two small islands and several rocks showing above water. **Inishmacsaint** has a jetty near the remains of a church. Close by is an early high cross—very tall, very plain, rather impressive. Early season visitors may care to check the legend that it rotates three times and bows to the rising sun on Easter morning. From the summit of the island is a fine view up and down the lake. It was here I encountered wild goats: a flock of twenty-five, led by a couple of old billys with immense curly horns.

The Catherine shoals are well marked and there is a black beacon central between markers 57 B, C, D and E which is visible from further away than the markers themselves. The south shore of the wide lake, though lacking in harbours, is sheltered from southerly winds by the mountains.

At the approach to the River Erne at the end of the lake I found many eel fishermen's nets. Coming out of the river, the first navigation markers appear round a sharp bend to starboard, while a deceptive stretch of open water ahead is a blind alley. From Rosscor viaduct 3 miles of dredged and dreary river lead between spoilt banks to Belleek. The dredging has altered the north bank of the river since the chart was made and there are now no islands along it.

At **Belleek** are two quays. The first, on the south bank, is in the entrance to a narrow creek, and has a fresh water supply. The other, on the north bank, is just above the bridge, by the village. A notice states that strong currents may occur here without warning—an effect of the hydroelectric power station downstream. The spit of land between the two quays

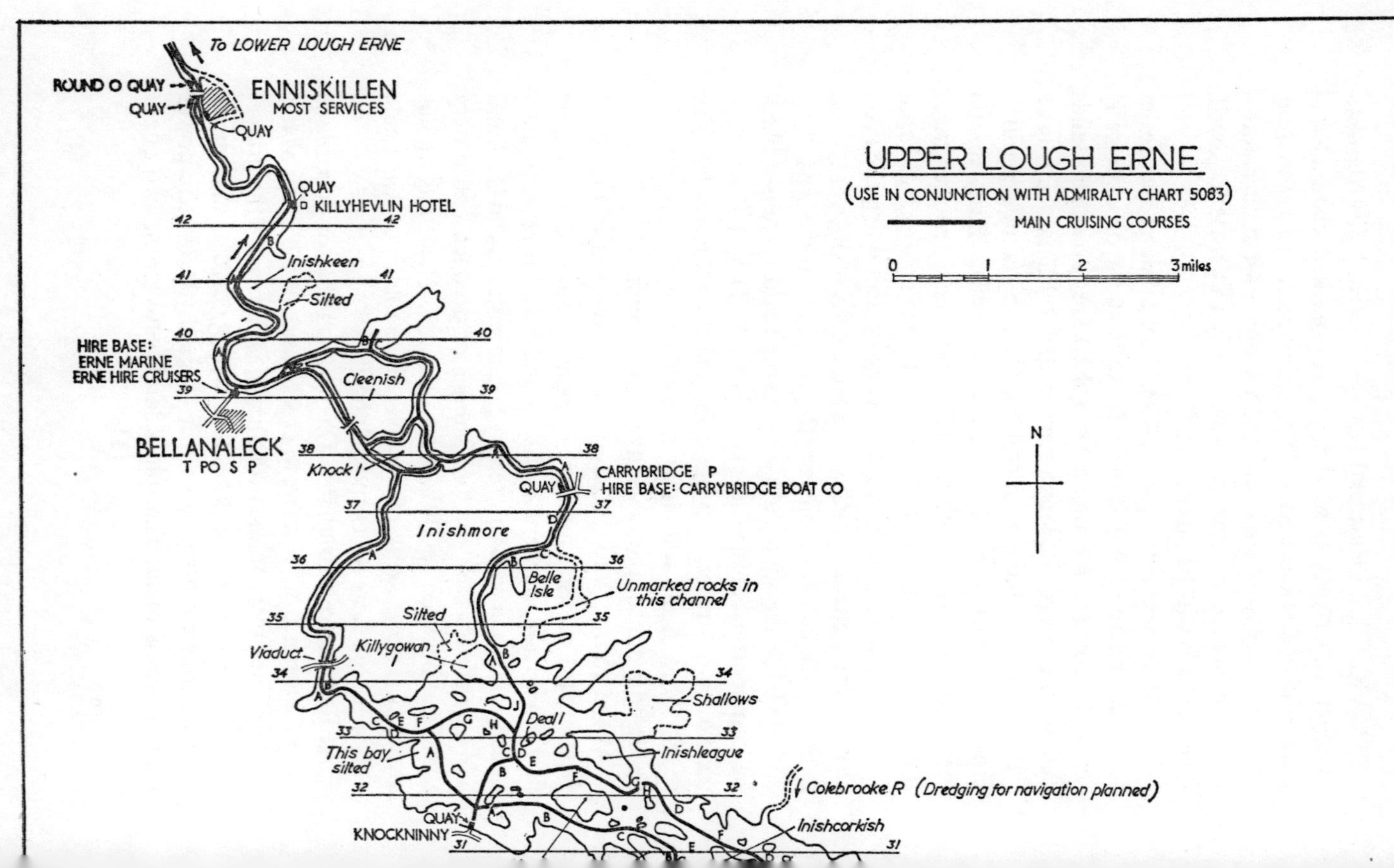
UPPER LOUGH ERNE
(USE IN CONJUNCTION WITH ADMIRALTY CHART 5083)
MAIN CRUISING COURSES
0 1 2 3 miles
N
To LOWER LOUGH ERNE
ROUND O QUAY
QUAY
ENNISKILLEN
MOST SERVICES
QUAY
QUAY
KILLYHEVLIN HOTEL
Inishkeen
Silted
HIRE BASE:
ERNE MARINE
ERNE HIRE CRUISERS
Cleenish I
BELLANALECK
T PO S P
Knock I
CARRYBRIDGE P
HIRE BASE: CARRYBRIDGE BOAT CO
QUAY
Inishmore
Belle Isle
Unmarked rocks in this channel
Silted
Killygowan I
Viaduct
Shallows
Deal I
This bay silted
Inishleague
Colebrooke R (Dredging for navigation planned)
QUAY
KNOCKNINNY
Inishcorkish

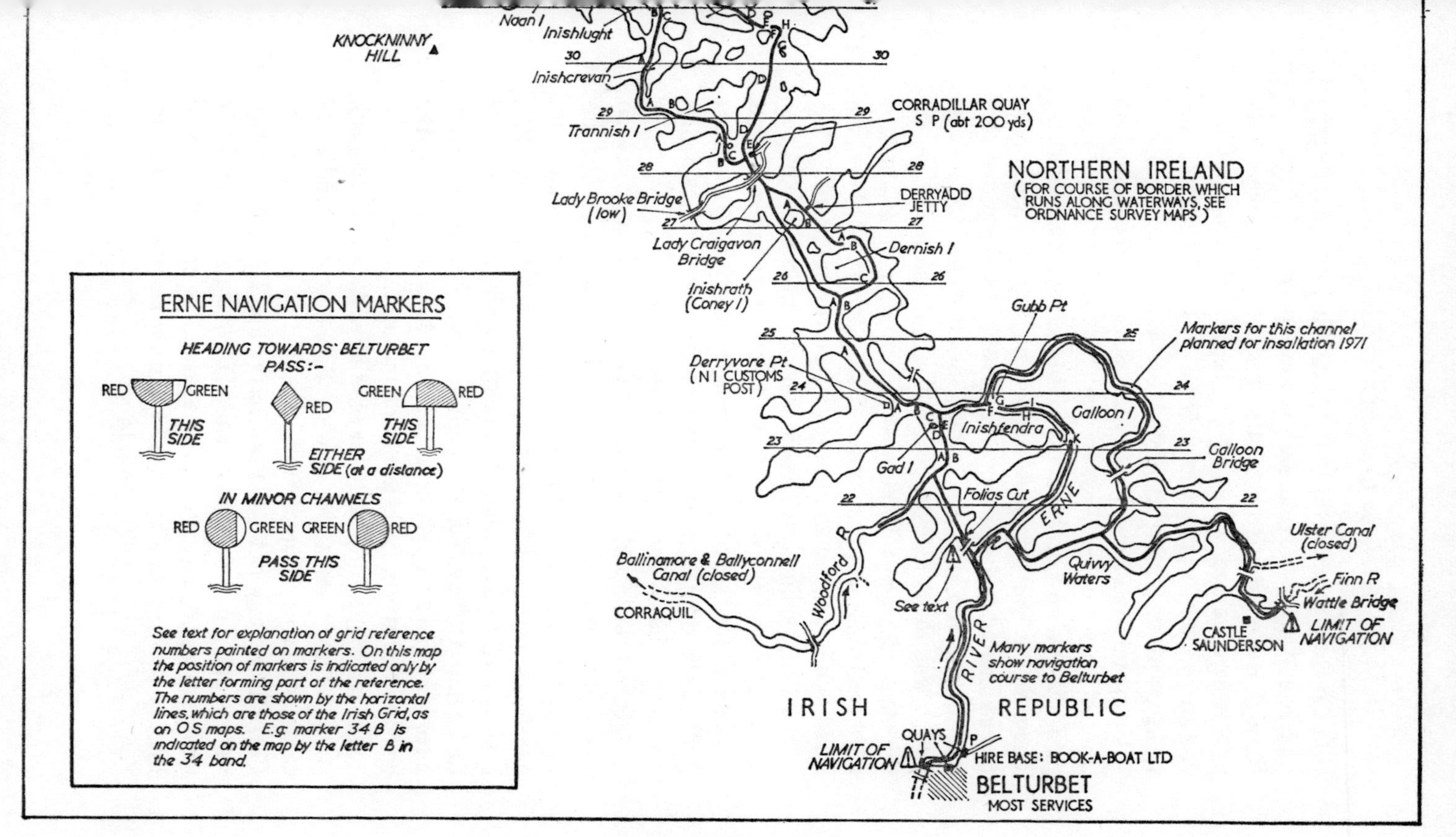
KNOCKNINNY HILL
Naan I
Inishlught
Inishcrevan
Trannish I
CORRADILLAR QUAY
S P (abt 200 yds)
NORTHERN IRELAND
(FOR COURSE OF BORDER WHICH RUNS ALONG WATERWAYS, SEE ORDNANCE SURVEY MAPS)
Lady Brooke Bridge (low)
DERRYADD JETTY
Lady Craigavon Bridge
Dernish I
Inishrath (Coney I)
Gubb Pt
Markers for this channel planned for insallation 1971
Derryvore Pt
(N I CUSTOMS POST)
Galloon I
Inishfendra
Gad I
Galloon Bridge
Folias Cut
ERNE
Ulster Canal (closed)
Ballinamore & Ballyconnell Canal (closed)
Woodford R
Quivvy Waters
Finn R
Wattle Bridge
CORRAQUIL
See text
CASTLE SAUNDERSON
LIMIT OF NAVIGATION
RIVER
Many markers show navigation course to Belturbet
IRISH REPUBLIC
QUAYS
LIMIT OF NAVIGATION
HIRE BASE: BOOK-A-BOAT LTD
BELTURBET
MOST SERVICES
ERNE NAVIGATION MARKERS
HEADING TOWARDS BELTURBET PASS:-
RED
GREEN
THIS SIDE
RED
EITHER SIDE (at a distance)
GREEN
RED
THIS SIDE
IN MINOR CHANNELS
RED
GREEN
GREEN
RED
PASS THIS SIDE
See text for explanation of grid reference numbers painted on markers. On this map the position of markers is indicated only by the letter forming part of the reference. The numbers are shown by the horizontal lines, which are those of the Irish Grid, as on O S maps. E.g. marker 34 B is indicated on the map by the letter B in the 34 band.

is in Co Donegal, and thus in the republic; it is permitted, I understand, to walk from the southern quay, round by road through the republic to cross the bridge to the village, back in Northern Ireland, without going through the Customs, but you are supposed not to stop on the way. The main part of the village, with its pottery and hotel, lies north of the bridge.

Upstream from Round O Quay, **Enniskillen**, the navigation channel passes under West Bridge; East Bridge is not navigable. Above West Bridge is a small island passable either side. There was a shortage of waterside fuelling installations at Enniskillen when I was there: a petrol station adjacent to a quay on the west bank above the bridge had closed. But I was told it was to be redeveloped, and a ¼ mile further on, on the same side, a petrol station visible from the river was having a creek dug out so that boats could approach it. There is a small public quay at Broadmeadow on the east bank.

The Killyhevlin Hotel has a pontoon moored to the east bank. The channel passes to the west of Inishkeen—what appears on the chart as a channel to the east is now silted. At **Bellanaleck** on the west bank are the bases of two hire operators; the village is 300yd up the road.

At Cleenish Island the channel divides and from here to Corradillar separate east and west channels are marked, although routes by which boats can cross from one to the other are shown on the Admiralty chart. At **Carrybridge** are jetties, a hotel and among other facilities the only waterside diesel fuel pump on the Erne, although hire craft operators usually have a waterside supply of diesel. The channel shown on the chart to the east of Belle Isle has unmarked rocks.

The landmark for **Knockninny** is a large round hill set back from the lake: at its foot is a good stone jetty extended recently in timber. There is road access but no facilities nearby. **Corradillar** quay is by the old ferry slip. There is a petrol station and small provisions shop 200yd up the road. Lady Craigavon bridge, east of Trasna Island, is navigable, Lady Brooke bridge to the west is low and the channel is shallow.

The Lisnaskea Boat Club and harbour is on the east shore, just north of **Derryadd**, which has a new county council jetty. The marked channel passes east of Inish Rath (or Coney Island) and Dernish Island but the shorter western channel is also navigable. At Gad Island with its little tower the channel splits again, the main and deeper course passing east of Inishfendra, while a shorter route heads south for Folias (or Foalies) Cut.

Half-way between Gad Island and Folias Cut, the Woodford River enters from the south-west; it once connected with the short-lived Ballinamore & Ballyconnell Canal to the Shannon. The approach from the lake is rather shallow but the river is navigable, I understand, to the remains of the first lock at Corraquil, at least when the water level is high. I cruised up the river for a mile or so. The border runs along its centre: one bank is in the North, the other in the republic, with no visible difference.

Folias Cut is artificial, probably built about the same time as the B & B Canal. It is not marked on the Admiralty chart, which preceded it. The depth of water is indicated on a board at each end; the cut is rather shallow. At its southern end it joins the main course which has followed the River Erne. There is yet a third way of reaching this point, for at Gubb Point, just up the river from Gad Island, a navigable channel wanders off round the east of Galloon Island, through the Quivvy Waters, and rejoins the main channel just downstream of the Folias Cut. Craft coming up the main channel here have to turn to starboard—there is a backwater straight ahead. Galloon Bridge crosses the channel east of Galloon Island—the second arch out from the east bank is marked for navigation.

A branch of the Quivvy Waters leads to the Finn River, navigable to within sight of Wattle Bridge. The mud- and weed-choked entrance to the long-closed Ulster Canal to the River Blackwater near Moy can be seen on the east bank, and in some bushes are the crumbling remains of its 26th Lock.

(This lock, by being the narrowest in Ireland, no doubt made its own particular contribution to the lack of viability of the nineteenth-century Neagh–Erne–Shannon through waterway.) Beyond the old canal entrance is a low bridge, and the corner in the river below Castle Saunderson I found to be shoaled. I moored to the north bank of a wide pool about 100yd below **Wattle Bridge**; intervening rapids were clear to see. There are no shops, no facilities, no quay, only a couple of farms.

The main channel continues from the entrance to the Folias Cut up to **Belturbet**. Book-a-boat's hire base is on the east bank at the approach to the town. A good new quay, and slipway a little further on on the same bank, are convenient for the centre of the town. The navigation continues until the river shoals about 50yd before Belturbet bridge—there is a small floating jetty on the west bank.

CHAPTER SEVEN

Lough Neagh and the Lower Bann Navigation[1]

Across Lough Neagh you see the curve in the earth's surface. The far side is about 11 miles away. Given a clear day and a good pair of binoculars, you can discern that rising ground is distinct, but the shore itself has dropped out of sight. From one end to the other, it is often impossible to see land at all; it is nearly 20 miles from the north-east corner to the south-west, and beyond that is another 20 miles or so of flat country.

From the lake the shores appear mostly low lying and it is possible to see the Antrim Mountains to the north-east, the Sperrin Mountains to the west and, sometimes, the Mourne Mountains far away to the south-east. The catchment area of Lough Neagh covers most of Northern Ireland—it is fed by six large rivers. The only outlet is the River Bann. The area of the lake itself is 153 sq miles, which makes it by a long way the biggest in Ireland, and it is roughly rectangular in shape with few islands. It seems more like the sea than an inland waterway; one wonders, momentarily, why the spray is not salt.

The sea illusion is heightened by shores of fine sand. Dredging sand from the lake bed for building is an important industry and sand barges, once steam but now all motor, go back and forth continuously. Despite this traffic, and a great many fishing craft, there has been no navigation authority,

[1] See pages 140 to 142 for strip maps of Lower Bann Navigation, River Blackwater and Upper Bann River.

generally speaking, since the abandonment in 1954 of the Upper Bann Navigation, which was responsible for most of the principal lake harbours. Only the approaches to the Lower Bann, at Toome, and the Six Mile Water, at Antrim, are maintained as part of the Lower Bann Navigation.

In the interests of drainage, the Northern Ireland Ministry of Agriculture (Drainage Division, York Buildings, 2 Curtis Street, Belfast BT1 2PF) maintains the level of the lake at 50ft to 50ft 6in above ordnance datum. In exceptional conditions it rises to 52ft or falls to about 49ft 7in. The ministry also dredges the Upper Bann and Blackwater Rivers for drainage. These rivers flow into the lake at its south-west corner, and formed part of the Upper Bann Navigation. So far as the abandoned navigation works are concerned, the ministry's responsibility is only to ensure that, by reason of their abandonment, they do not cause damage to property or become a danger to the public.

Local authorities around the lake, which is bordered by five of the six Northern counties, are aware of its amenity value, and are taking an interest in the restoration and maintenance of harbours. The whole of the south shore of the lake is within the designated area for the new city of Craigavon (based on Lurgan and Portadown) and planners have set it aside for recreation and amenity. There is no restriction on placing boats on the lake, and there is a good new slipway at Oxford Island (Lough Neagh Yacht Club), and a smaller one at Maghery (Maghery Motor Boat and Sailing Club). The number of privately owned pleasure craft on the lake is increasing, but there are at present no hire craft on either the lake or the Lower Bann. They will probably be introduced in time.

Unfortunately the full potential of Lough Neagh for holiday cruising is likely to remain potential in the absence of an up-to-date hydrographic survey—the Craigavon Development Commission has made a good start in its sector of the lake—followed by installation of clearly understandable markers to indicate the approach channels to the main sheltered harbours. At present there is no single system of marking obstructions in use throughout the lake, and since the Admiralty chart (no 5074) was published in 1835 successive drainage schemes have lowered the water level by about 4ft. Rocky shoals, called 'flats' here, have become islands and the shoreline has altered. It is, I believe, shown accurately on one-inch scale Northern Ireland Ordnance Survey maps sheets 5 and 6. In the circumstances it is difficult to give worthwhile navigation instructions, but I hope the notes below will be of some value, and I recommend any stranger to the lake to seek as much local advice as possible before setting out; I have found the River Bann Association particularly helpful. It plans to publish a new boating guide to the area in 1970.

The centre of the lake is generally free from hazards such as shoals or rocks, but the lake has a reputation for rough weather which may blow up in a quarter of an hour. I saw force eight equinoctial gales produce handsome breakers in the mouth of the Six Mile Water, but was told it was the worst weather for seven months. Big waves come in threes, called the three sisters. Traditional open fishing boats, designed no doubt from experience of bad weather, are high bowed and about 22ft long. The lake bottom is generally gravelly, and gives good holding for anchors; but rocky points and flats shelve only very gently beneath the surface and are best given a wide berth. When cruising parallel to the shore, local advice is to keep ½ mile or so off, and to come into harbours at right angles. For a short time in the late spring, Lough Neagh suffers from a plague of flies, which I have not had the misfortune to encounter.

The navigational vacuum of Lough Neagh is all the more to be regretted when compared with its link to the sea, the Lower Bann Navigation from Toome to Coleraine. This is well maintained but little used. Apart from a short section at Toome used by sand barges, perhaps twenty craft a month pass along this navigation in summer, fewer in winter. That it is maintained at all is due to an enlightened awareness of the navigation authority, the Ministry of Agriculture, of its amenity value (prodded, no doubt, by the River Bann Association). The number of craft on the waterway is slowly increasing.

The non-tidal part of the navigation runs for about 30 miles from Toome northwards to The Cutts, near Coleraine, and also includes ½ mile of the Six Mile Water. It appears on one-inch scale Northern Ireland Ordnance Survey maps sheets 1, 2, 3 and 6. A little way below Toome it passes through Lough Beg; for the rest of the way to The Cutts it is a broad river, with occasional side canals and locks, which passes through a countryside of farms and forestry. Many of the plantations were originally spoil tips from drainage operations in the 1930s. The bottom of the river is gravel with rock outcrops: the banks are often soft enough to moor to.

The channel is indicated by markers, which are posts with a pointer on top to indicate the side that boats are to pass, and notices on the banks which state, for instance, that boats are to keep so many feet out from the bank until the next lock. These notices refer to left and right bank in relation to direction of travel. In the absence of any indication to the contrary, the channel follows the centre of the river. Locks can accommodate craft up to 110ft by 19ft 6in beam; the maximum draught is normally 5ft 6in, but low water sometimes reduces this to 4ft 6in. The locks are operated only by lock-keepers, whose official hours of work are 9.0 am to 6.0 pm throughout the week, although it may be possible to pass through out of hours by arrangement with individual lock-keepers. The lock fee for pleasure craft is 5p (1s), but as this nominal charge has been unaltered for some seventy years it seems unlikely to remain stable indefinitely. The first lock-keeper encountered issues a boat with a permit for the whole of its intended journey. As lock-keepers have other duties, it is customary for people intending to cruise along the navigation, to avoid delay, to telephone the keeper of the first lock that they will come to and tell him their expected arrival time. Each lock-keeper in turn telephones forward to the next. Telephone numbers of lock-keepers appear in the telephone directory under 'Government of Northern Ireland—Ministry of Agriculture—Bann Drainage'. A programme of lock gate replacement is at present being carried out; renewals are made, so far as possible, in spring or autumn, between the main flood and cruising seasons.

Most bridges have a swing span adjacent to one of the banks, through which the navigation channel passes. Swing spans can be opened, if necessary, free of charge, by prior application to the Area Engineer, Ministry of Agriculture Drainage Division, The Cutts, Coleraine, Co Londonderry. The current in the river is normally less than four knots. But after heavy rain it is necessary to open floodgates at Portna and The Cutts: there is then a strong current above the floodgates and at such times navigation is dangerous between Hutchinson's Ford and Portna and between Loughan Island and The Cutts. This happens occasionally in summer, frequently in winter. Lock-keepers know the state of the river, and skippers in any doubt are advised to contact the area engineer's office. If a passage is essential during these flood conditions, it may be possible to arrange with the area engineer for floodgates to be closed temporarily: but navigation has to take its turn with conflicting considerations of flooding, fisheries and bank slippage. The map of Lough Neagh is on p 124.

I launched my boat down the ramp into the Six Mile Water at the Royal Engineers' bridging camp at **Antrim**, by kind permission of the commanding officer. Near the mouth of this river, the north bank is occupied by moorings of the Antrim Boat Club. The south bank has a slipway, a small quay and a car park (improvements were planned by Antrim County Council); the town is ¾ mile up the road. There is also another small quay from which the *Maid of Antrim* runs cruises on the lake.

The approach to the river, dredged recently to 3ft 6in, is

between a pair of markers, one of which still carried a large white diamond topmark although the other, which previously had one, has lost it. From out in the bay, an indication of the position of the river mouth is a large white rectangular building which rises behind the trees. Immediately to the northwest of the river mouth is a large torpedo-testing structure—a relic of the war—which obstructs the bay.

On the way to Toome the main hazard is the island called Skady Tower on the Admiralty chart (no tower, only bushes) and rocks nearby. Going to Toome, locals do not turn north until they can see the floodgates in the distance (they look like a bridge, with six concrete uprights), and going to Antrim, they continue south until Skady closes with the north shore before turning east. The entrance to the **Toome Canal** is on the east shore, ½ mile short of the weir, rather difficult to spot, except by heading as if into Brockish Bay when it opens up to port; there are markers, without topmarks, one each side of the entrance. (Strip maps of Lower Bann Navigation commence on p 140.)

Toome Canal with its lock, smart in green and white paint, is something most unusual in Ireland—a busy commercial waterway. Sand barges pass through about fifteen times a day, and, moored above the lock, I found little chance of sleep after 7 am. It seemed a paradox that this should be so on a navigation which, for most of its length and history, has been a commercial failure: for by the time the Lower Bann Navigation was completed in 1859 a parallel railway was already open. At Toome, most pleasure craft moor to the east bank above the first bridge, formerly rail, now road, with its navigation arch adjacent to the east bank. Two quays between this and the next, main road, bridge (navigation arch again next east bank) are public but usually full of sand barges.

After 1½ miles of river the channel enters Lough Beg. The lake is shallow, ornithologically famous, and has a shoreline much altered since the Admiralty chart was made. The channel, narrow and perhaps uncomfortable in a cross wind, runs between closely spaced pairs of posts. Many of those along the east side of the channel have triangular topmarks (pass the side that the triangle points). In the distance Lough Beg looks like nothing so much as an inundated golf course!

At **Newferry**, on the east bank, is the base of the Newferry Boating and Water Ski Club; the ferry slipway adjoining has been concreted for launching boats. A little further on, on the the west bank, is the factory of the Diatomite Company, which uses barge transport to connect its workings along the river where diatomite earth is dug from the banks.

At Portglenone Forest, a new quay is an invitation to stop for a while at this pleasant, secluded, spot. **Portglenone** itself, though not large, is the main town on the non-tidal river. Its bridge has a swing navigation arch adjacent to the east bank, with a quay immediately downstream. The Bridge Inn, close by, had plans for developments here.

It is a longish but pleasant cruise to **Hutchinson's Ford,** where there is a small timber quay on the west bank which looks as though it may be too shallow for large craft. A notice advises craft to keep within 50ft of the west bank until the entrance to the **Portna Canal**; the floodgates are immediately down river beyond the canal entrance. The canal leads through a short but deep rock cutting to Portna double lock; the canal immediately above the lock can be drained to provide a dry dock (and block the navigation) but this is now seldom done.

Just below **Kilrea** bridge (swing navigation span next east bank) is a quay. The town is a mile away to the west. The entrance to the **Movanagher Canal** is on the east bank, with an open weir immediately downstream. This lock and the next at Carnroe are worked by the same lock-keeper. Across Movanagher Lock chamber is a swing bridge, worked by the lock-keeper if necessary, which gives access to Movanagher fish farm. Here $1\frac{1}{4}$ million fish, mainly trout and salmon, are bred each year to stock fishing waters throughout Northern

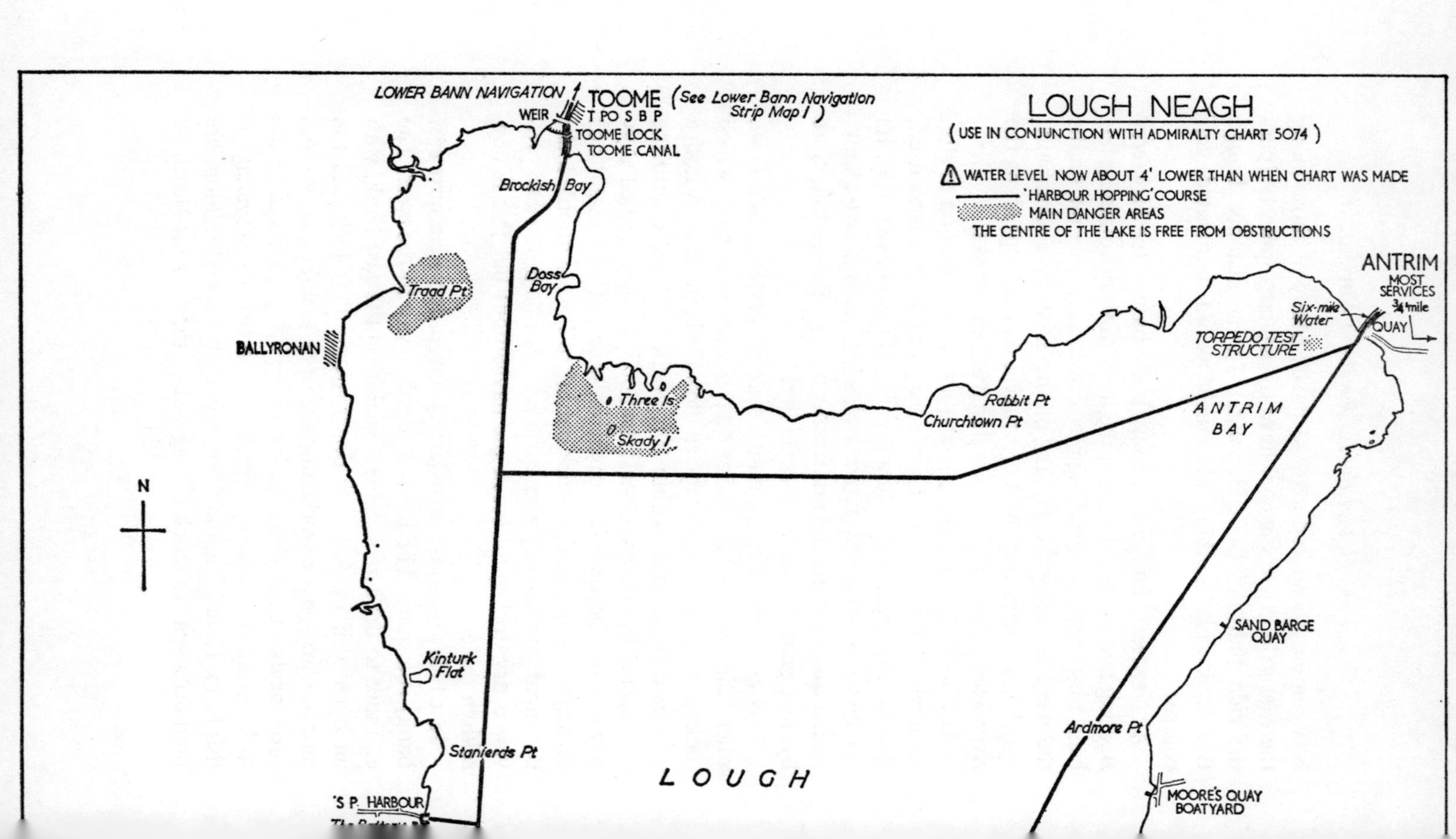
LOUGH NEAGH
(USE IN CONJUNCTION WITH ADMIRALTY CHART 5074)
WATER LEVEL NOW ABOUT 4' LOWER THAN WHEN CHART WAS MADE
'HARBOUR HOPPING' COURSE
MAIN DANGER AREAS
THE CENTRE OF THE LAKE IS FREE FROM OBSTRUCTIONS
LOWER BANN NAVIGATION
TOOME (See Lower Bann Navigation Strip Map I)
T PO S B P
WEIR
TOOME LOCK
TOOME CANAL
Brockish Bay
Doss Bay
Traad Pt
BALLYRONAN
Three Is
Skady I
Rabbit Pt
Churchtown Pt
ANTRIM
MOST SERVICES
¾ mile
QUAY
Six-mile Water
TORPEDO TEST STRUCTURE
ANTRIM BAY
N
SAND BARGE QUAY
Ardmore Pt
MOORE'S QUAY BOATYARD
Kinturk Flat
Stanierds Pt
LOUGH
'S P. HARBOUR

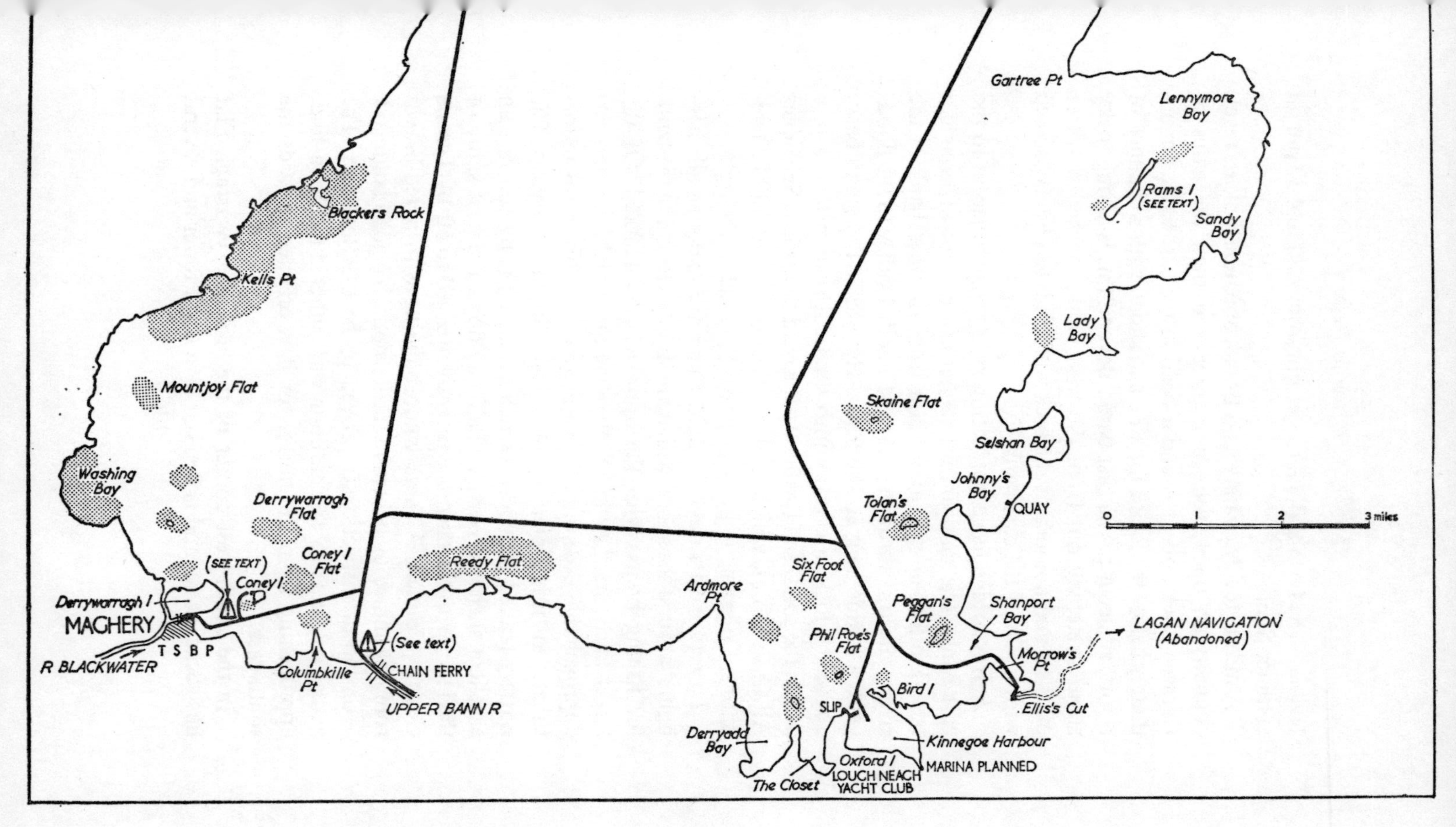
Gartree Pt
Lennymore Bay
Rams I (SEE TEXT)
Sandy Bay
Lady Bay
Blackers Rock
Kells Pt
Mountjoy Flat
Skaine Flat
Selshan Bay
Johnny's Bay
QUAY
0
1
2
3 miles
Washing Bay
Derrywarragh Flat
Tolan's Flat
Reedy Flat
(SEE TEXT)
Coney I Flat
Coney I
Six Foot Flat
Ardmore Pt
Peggan's Flat
Shanport Bay
Derrywarragh I
MAGHERY
LAGAN NAVIGATION (Abandoned)
Phil Roe's Flat
Morrow's Pt
(See text)
T S B P
R BLACKWATER
Columbkille Pt
CHAIN FERRY
Bird I
SLIP
Ellis's Cut
UPPER BANN R
Derryadd Bay
Kinnegoe Harbour
Oxford I
LOUGH NEAGH YACHT CLUB
MARINA PLANNED
The Closet

Ireland. The farm is open to visitors from 2.30 to 4.30 pm on summer Sundays.

A mile below Movanagher a broad, apparently clear, reach contains an open weir—a marker and then the gates of **Carnroe Lock** appear round a bend in the east bank. Immediately below the lock I found a bad shoal, with a channel, of a sort, adjacent to the east bank. Beyond this is a long rocky shoal stretching out from the west bank, marked by three markers and a notice at the lock which advises boats to keep within 50ft of the east bank.

Agivey bridge has a navigation swing span adjacent to the east bank. The navigation channel passes west of Loughan Island and then runs about 30ft from the west bank of the river as it flows through a narrow wooded valley to the flood-gates and tide lock at **The Cutts.** Here there is a small basin above the lock, a slipway into the tidal river below, a pub across the road, and further up the road to the left, Selfridges All Cash Stores, which is also a post office with public telephone. Coleraine is 1½ miles down the road to the right.

To return to Lough Neagh: there are many small 'harbours' around the shore, which are simply slits cut in the bank for fishing boats, with the approaches unmarked. Of the larger harbours, I found **Ballyronan** quay high, dry and unapproachable except, perhaps, by dinghy. This seems unfortunate, for it is a picturesque village with most services. **The Battery** (called Newport Trench on maps) is by contrast an excellent sheltered harbour half-way down the west shore of the lake, with the entrance recently dredged to 6ft by Tyrone County Council. A large white building with a red-brown roof, set immediately behind the harbour, is a good landmark —on closer inspection it proved to be the Boat Inn. The actual entrance to the harbour was rather difficult to find, approaching from the north, for it is oriented towards the south-east.

In the south-west corner of the lake, Derrywarragh Flat has rocks awash and is marked by a small tower and several stone beacons. Coney Island Flat has rocks, covered with grass, above the water, and also is marked with stone beacons; but I found this flat most difficult to spot when approaching from the north-east—it merges with Coney Island proper. Off Columbkille point was a large black perch with a hoop topmark, installed, I would guess, by the Upper Bann Navigation at a time when the water level was higher. **Coney Island** has a jetty on the west side used by the *Maid of Antrim*, but to reach it, after passing south of the island, it is necessary first to pass west of a small red buoy, installed by the Maghery Motor Boat and Sailing Club, which marks the extremity of a shoal stretching south-west from the island. Coney Island itself is small and wooded, National Trust property, once a haunt of St Patrick.

The approach to the **Maghery Canal**, up the shallow and weedy unnamed bay in front of the village, was not, I found, straightforward. The mouth of the canal is in the north-west corner of the bay, but the route to it is to steer a mid-course, towards the squat-towered church on its low hill, until pairs of small red buoys, installed by the MMB & SC, open up to starboard. The channel lies between them. The Maghery Canal, though shallow at the edges, provides very sheltered moorings; Craigavon has great plans for boating developments here, including improvements to the low bridge which at present spans the canal half-way between the lake and the River Blackwater. It is possible to leave Maghery by going down the Blackwater and to the north of Derrywarragh Island, but having put my boat on the rocks while attempting to find this route I am disinclined to recommend it! (The strip map of River Blackwater is on p 142.)

Dredging has made the first few miles of the River Blackwater rather dreary, as spoil has been piled along the banks. The abandoned Coalisland Canal appears derelict. There is a small quay on the east bank of the river just below Verners Bridge, and a large tributary enters on the same side just above the bridge. From a little way above Verners Bridge to

Moy the river winds between low green hills, farms and woodland; it is to be hoped that the dredging planned will not spoil this stretch of delightful waterway. The banks are mostly soft and there were a few boats moored at Bonds Bridge. On the east bank ½ mile before Moy is the derelict entrance lock to the closed Ulster Canal. I moored to the west bank a little below **Moy** bridge. The main part of the picturesque little town is up the road to the right, grouped formally and placidly around its broad tree-lined main street. Small boats can continue up the river, I understand, until about 50yd below **Blackwatertown** bridge.

The entrance to the Upper Bann River from Lough Neagh is marked by posts. Unfortunately no indication survives of which side you are intended to pass them. Trial and error found a satisfactory course by first leaving to port a black perch, well out in the lake and similar to that off Columbkille point; and then leaving to port: a post with two stumps adjacent, and two further stumps at intervals; and to starboard: a stake with a rectangular topmark and a post close together, and another post further on. The next hazard was the Bannfoot ferry, a fine and busy example of a 'chain ferry' worked by two ropes stretched beside one another taut across the river about 4ft 6in above water level. It must, presumably, be possible to raise or lower them for large craft, for there were sand barges up the river which would necessitate this. There is a small quay on each bank immediately downstream of the ferry, and **Bannfoot** village is ½ mile up the road on the east bank. (Upper Bann River strip map is on p 142.)

The river is broad, rather weedy close to soft banks, and winds through generally flat country. A little below the M1 motorway bridge is a sand barge quay on the east bank. I found little to welcome the cruising visitor to **Portadown**; a few boats were moored to the east bank between new and old road bridges behind a securely padlocked gate, and shallow-draught craft could probably moor to a patch of waste ground opposite; however, boating amenities are included in the Craigavon plan for this area. Portadown itself is an industrial town of some 21,000 inhabitants and its shops should be able to supply most boaters' needs.

Along the south shore of Lough Neagh, I have been recommended to keep well off Reedy Flat and Ardmore point. Six Foot Flat (unnamed on the Admiralty chart, but with soundings 9, 6, 9) is marked by a post with a barrel topmark; as the Craigavon chart for this area shows shallows to the south, the best course for visitors heading for the bay called **Kinnegoe Harbour** is probably to pass north of Six Foot Flat and east of Phil Roe's Flat, which is visible above water. The spires of two churches at Lurgan are good landmarks. A new breakwater stretches out from the north-east corner of Oxford Island (now only a promontory) and a stake marks a shallow between it and the opposite shore of the bay. The new slipway is just outside the breakwater and new moorings for the Lough Neagh Yacht Club just inside; the south shore of the bay is to be developed as a marina.

Peggans and Tolans Flats are both visible above water; Skaine Flat has a marker of some sort, said to be the remains of a sand barge: not wishing to add my own boat I did not go close enough to examine in detail! Heading for the entrance to the closed Lagan Navigation, which used to connect the lake with Belfast, I left a post off Morrows Point to starboard and then kept close to the south shore of Shanport Bay to find the canal entrance in the reeds. It is called **Ellis's Cut** and is a sheltered mooring; there may be some minor developments here by Craigavon.

Bad weather obliged me to cut short my visit to the east side of Lough Neagh. **Ram's Island** has, I understand, a sheltered jetty on the east side, best approached from the south, but car-borne visits showed the quays in Sandy Bay to be either private or derelict. There is a rough quay in **Johnny's Bay**, with signs of occasional use by sand barges, and McGarry's boatyard is at **Moores Quay**.

A Note about Lake Maps

On lake maps included in the text, symbols used to indicate services available at villages (T, PO, etc) are the same as those used on the strip maps, explained opposite. So are the symbols for lock, weir, hazard, direction of current, bridge, town or village, and railway.

Shores shown by a dotted line are of areas which are either un-navigable or at least not recommended.

Navigation courses and markers have required individual treatment on each waterway; they are explained on each map.

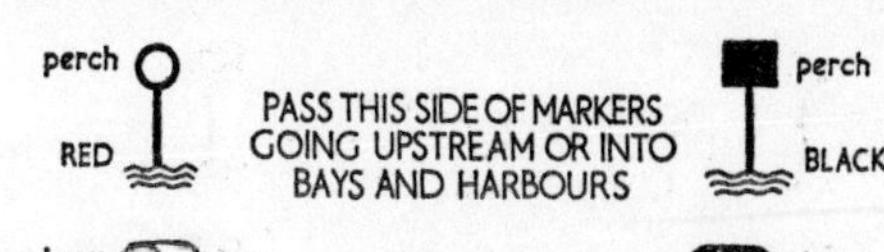

KEY TO STRIP MAPS

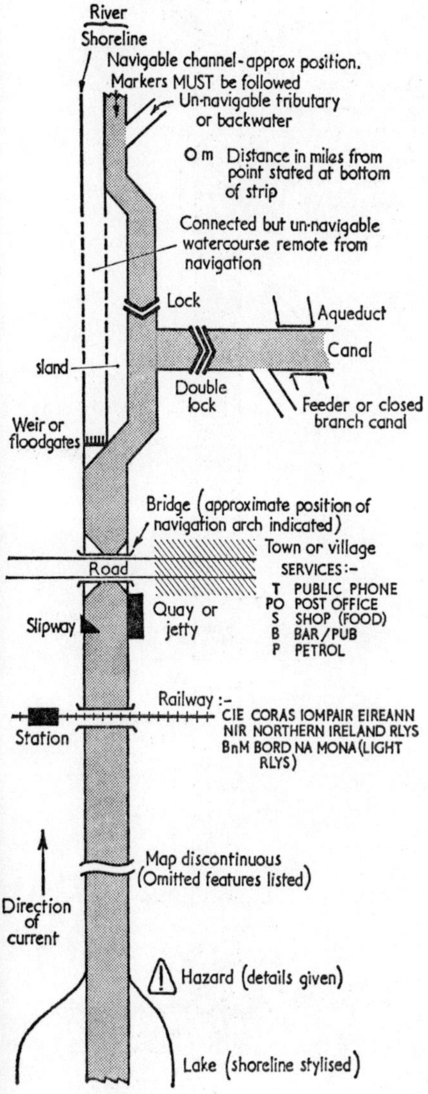

River
Shoreline
Navigable channel - approx position.
Markers MUST be followed
Un-navigable tributary or backwater
O m Distance in miles from point stated at bottom of strip
Connected but un-navigable watercourse remote from navigation
Lock
Aqueduct
Canal
sland
Double lock
Feeder or closed branch canal
Weir or floodgates
Bridge (approximate position of navigation arch indicated)
Road
Town or village
SERVICES:-
T PUBLIC PHONE
PO POST OFFICE
S SHOP (FOOD)
B BAR/PUB
P PETROL
Quay or jetty
Slipway
Railway :-
CIE CORAS IOMPAIR EIREANN
NIR NORTHERN IRELAND RLYS
BnM BORD NA MONA (LIGHT RLYS)
Station
Map discontinuous (Omitted features listed)
Direction of current
Hazard (details given)
Lake (shoreline stylised)

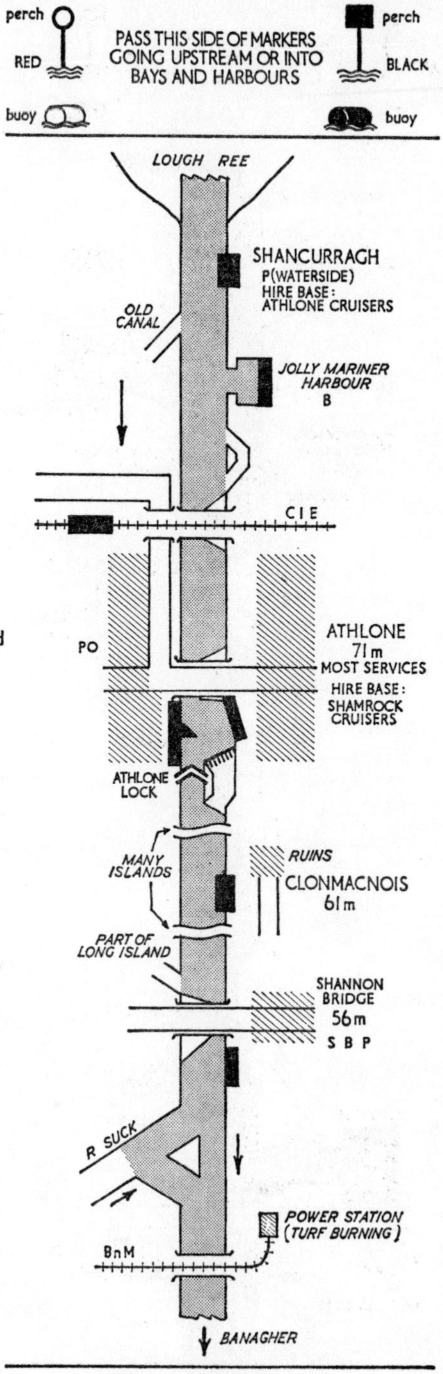

perch
RED
buoy
PASS THIS SIDE OF MARKERS GOING UPSTREAM OR INTO BAYS AND HARBOURS
perch
BLACK
buoy
LOUGH REE
SHANCURRAGH
P(WATERSIDE)
HIRE BASE:
ATHLONE CRUISERS
OLD CANAL
JOLLY MARINER HARBOUR
B
CIE
ATHLONE
71 m
MOST SERVICES
HIRE BASE:
SHAMROCK CRUISERS
PO
ATHLONE LOCK
MANY ISLANDS
RUINS
CLONMACNOIS
61 m
PART OF LONG ISLAND
SHANNON BRIDGE
56 m
S B P
R SUCK
POWER STATION (TURF BURNING)
BnM
BANAGHER

SHANNON NAVIGATION I

Distances in miles from Ardnacrusha

See pp 41, 48

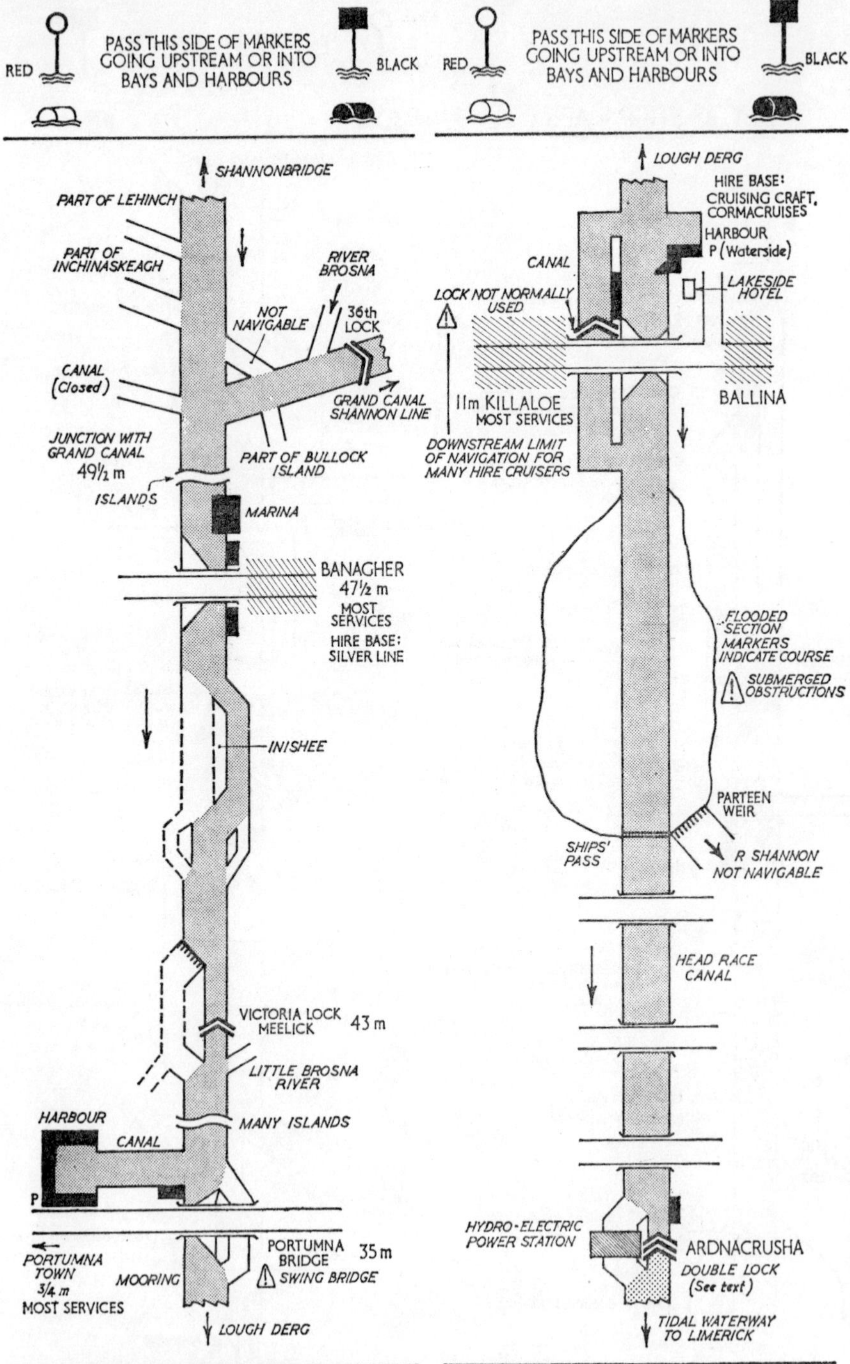

SHANNON NAVIGATION 2

Distances in miles from Ardnacrusha

See pp 42–3

SHANNON NAVIGATION 3

Distances in miles from Ardnacrusha

See pp 45–8

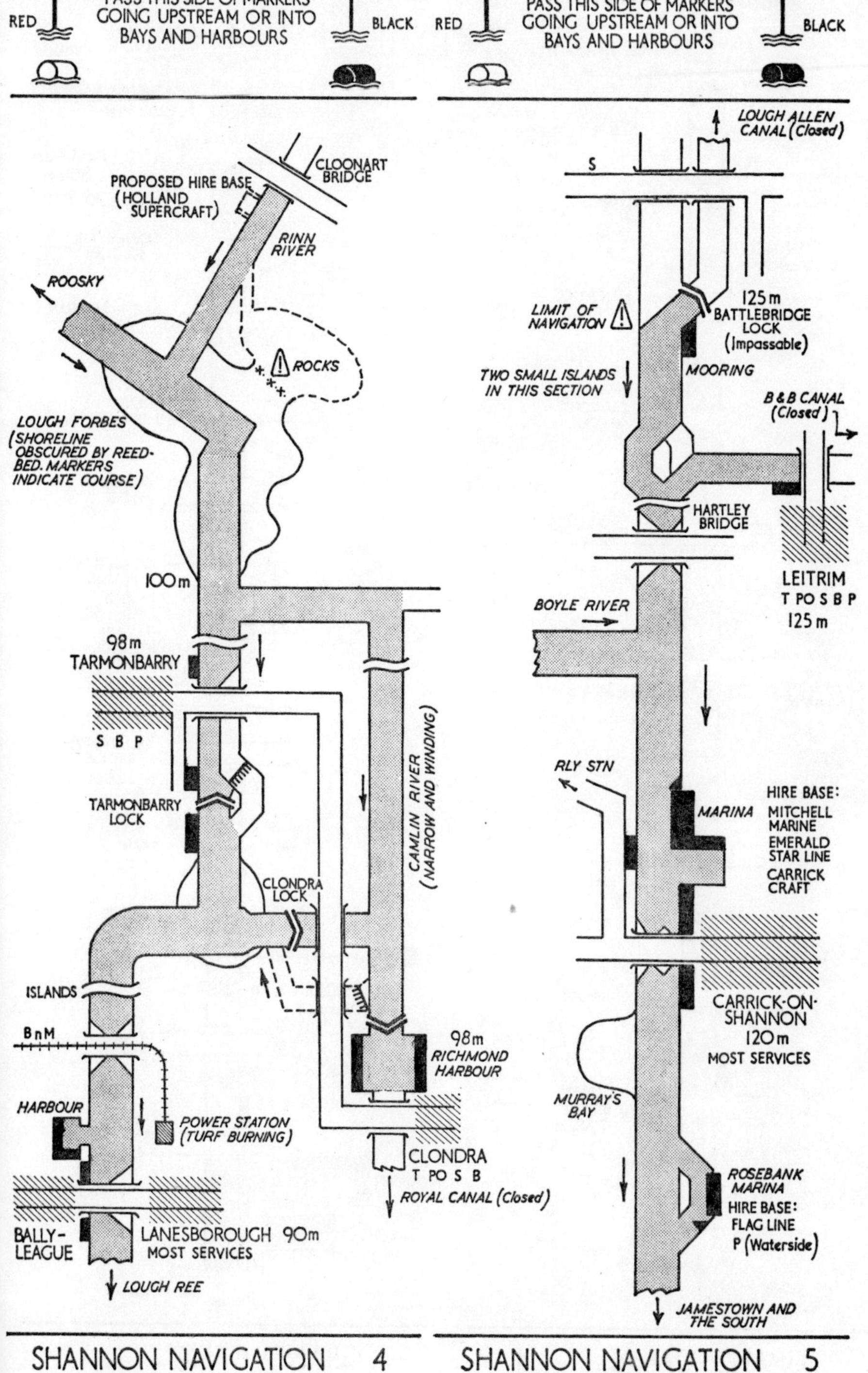

SHANNON NAVIGATION 4

Distances in miles from Ardnacrusha

See pp 53–5

SHANNON NAVIGATION 5

Distances in miles from Ardnacrusha

See pp 59–60

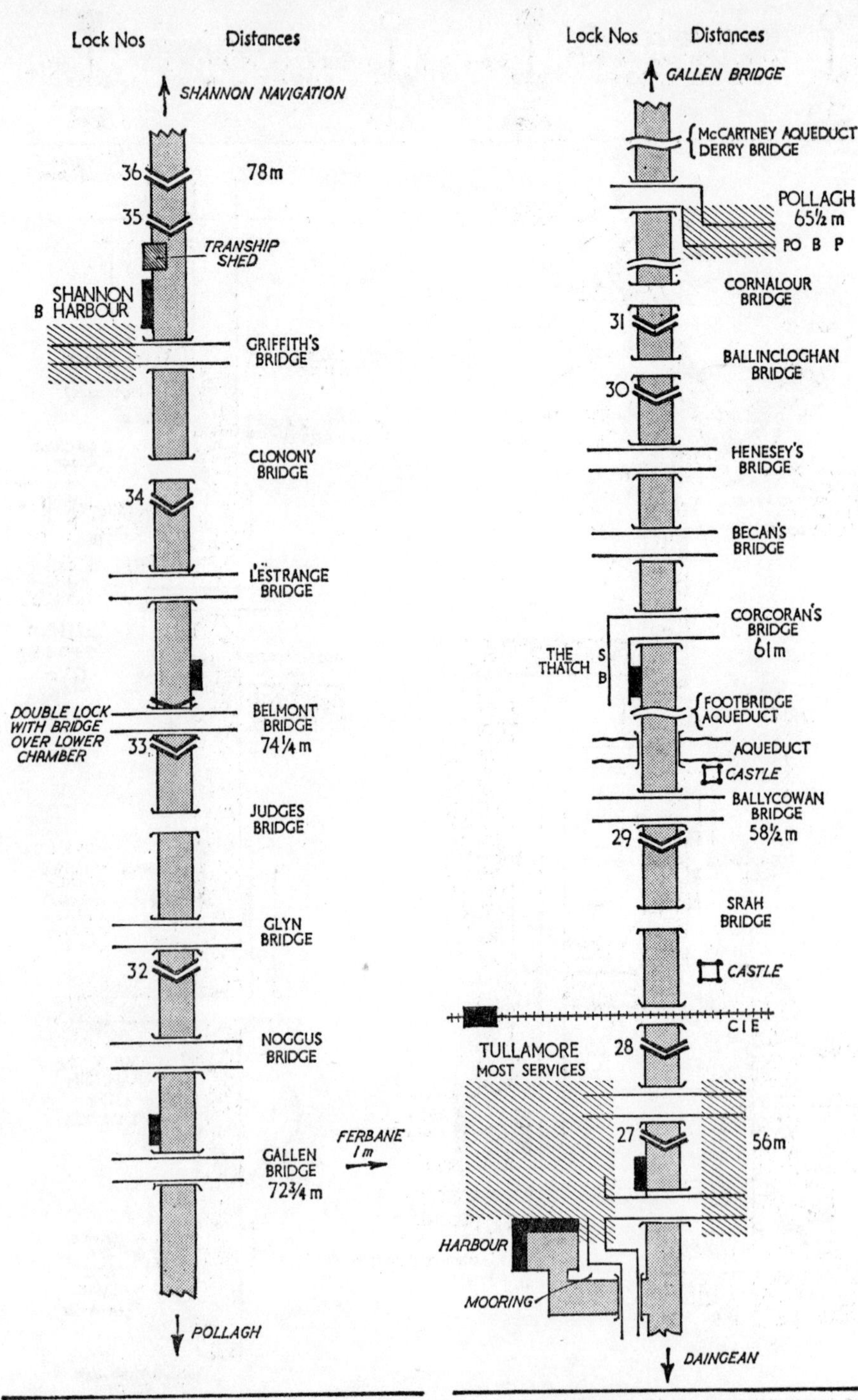

GRAND CANAL 1

Distances in miles from First Lock

See pp 68–9

GRAND CANAL 2

Distances in miles from First Lock

See pp 69–70

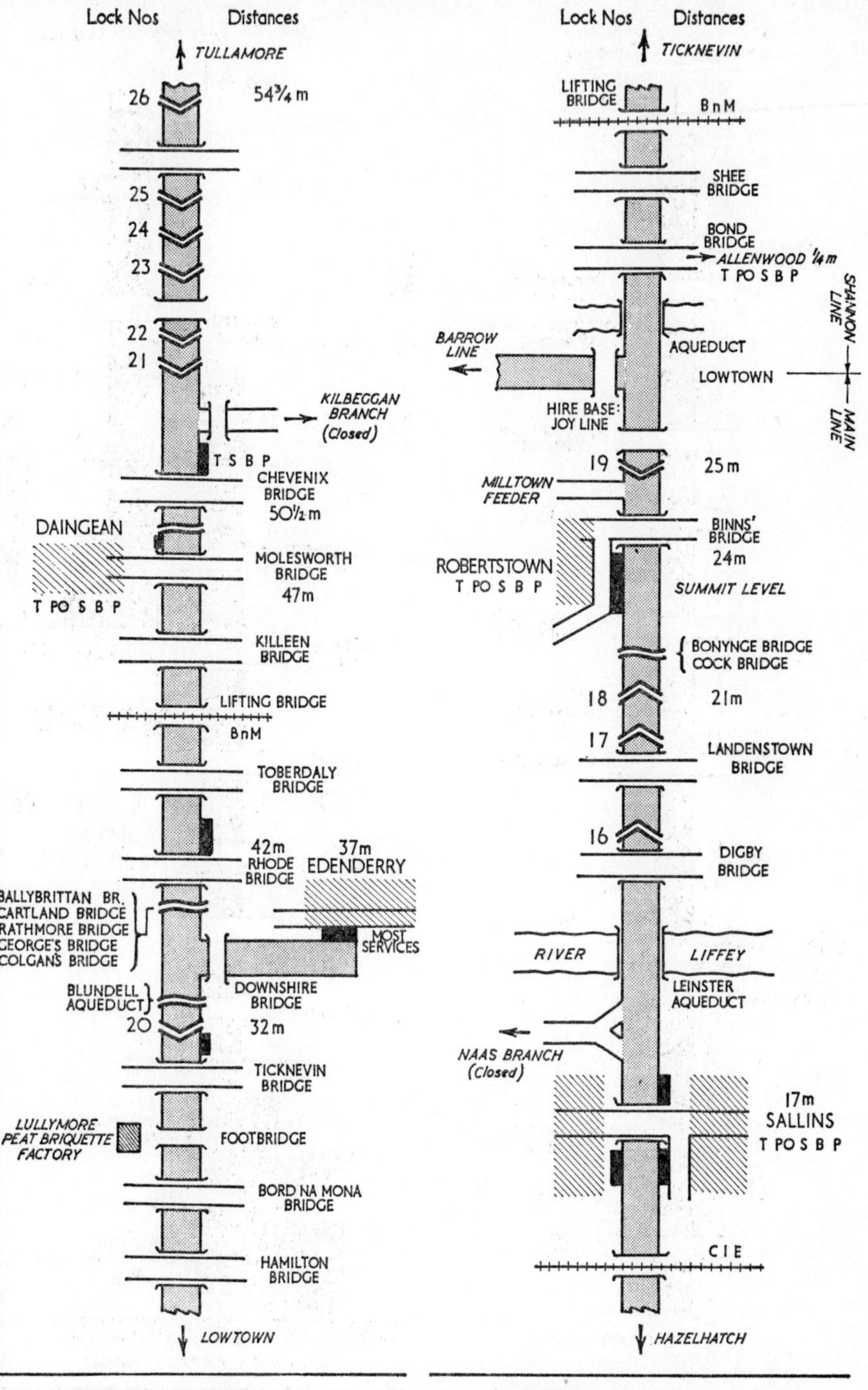

GRAND CANAL 3

Distances in miles from First Lock

See pp 70–1

GRAND CANAL 4

Distances in miles from First Lock

See pp 71–3

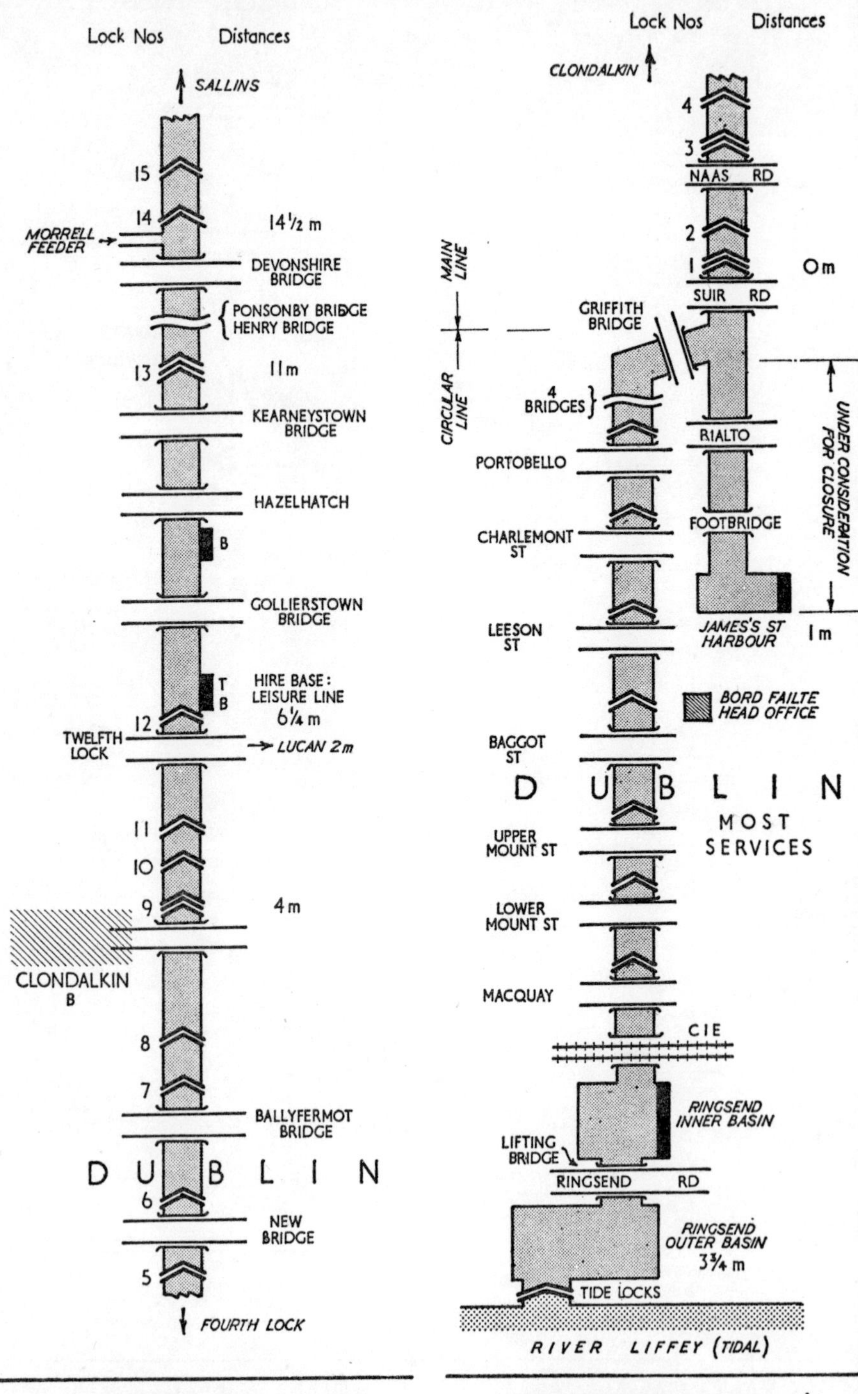

GRAND CANAL 5

Distances in miles from First Lock

See pp 73–5

GRAND CANAL 6

Distances in miles from First Lock

See pp 75–7

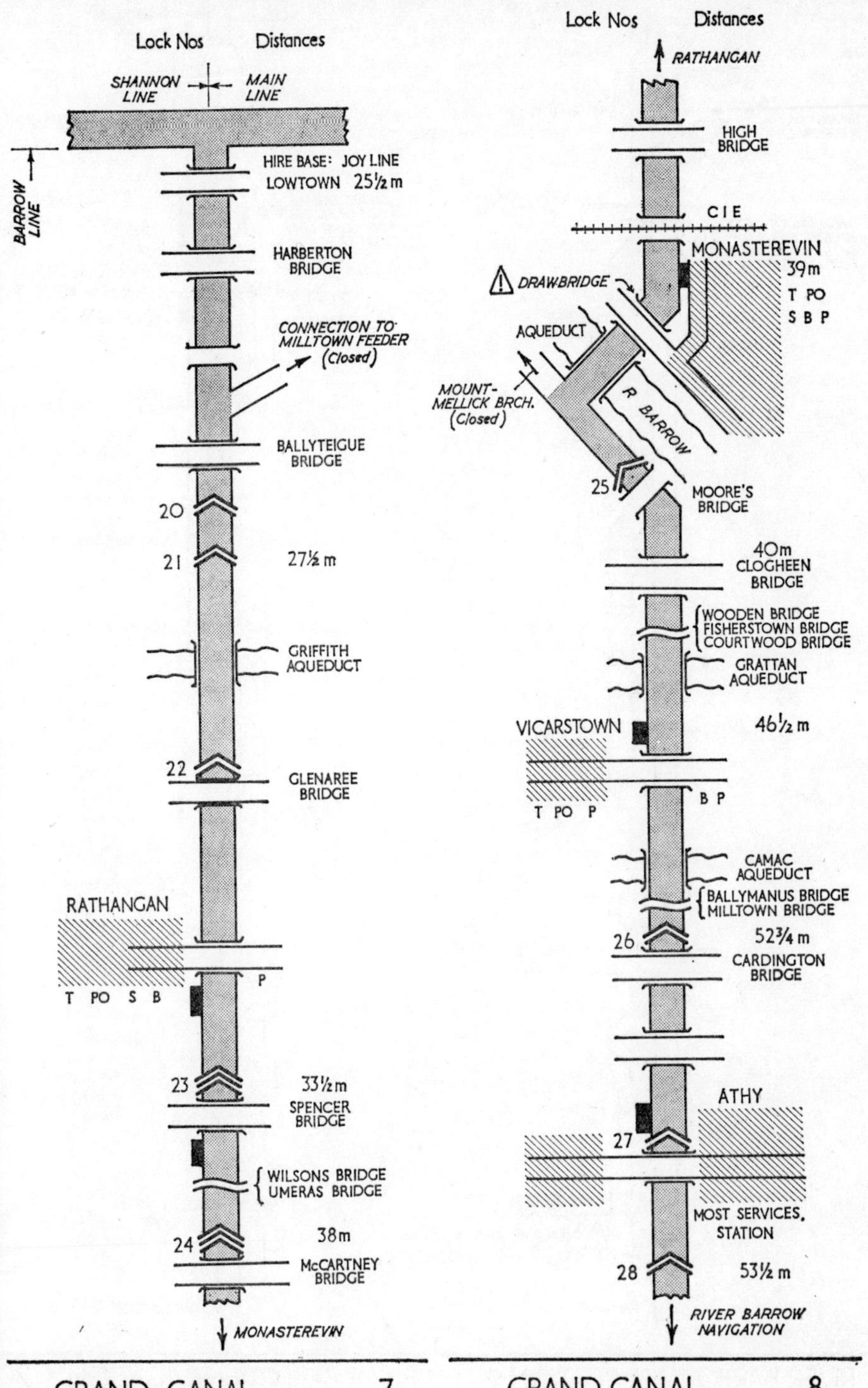

GRAND CANAL 7

Distances in miles from First Lock

See pp 77–8

GRAND CANAL 8

Distances in miles from First Lock

See pp 78–9

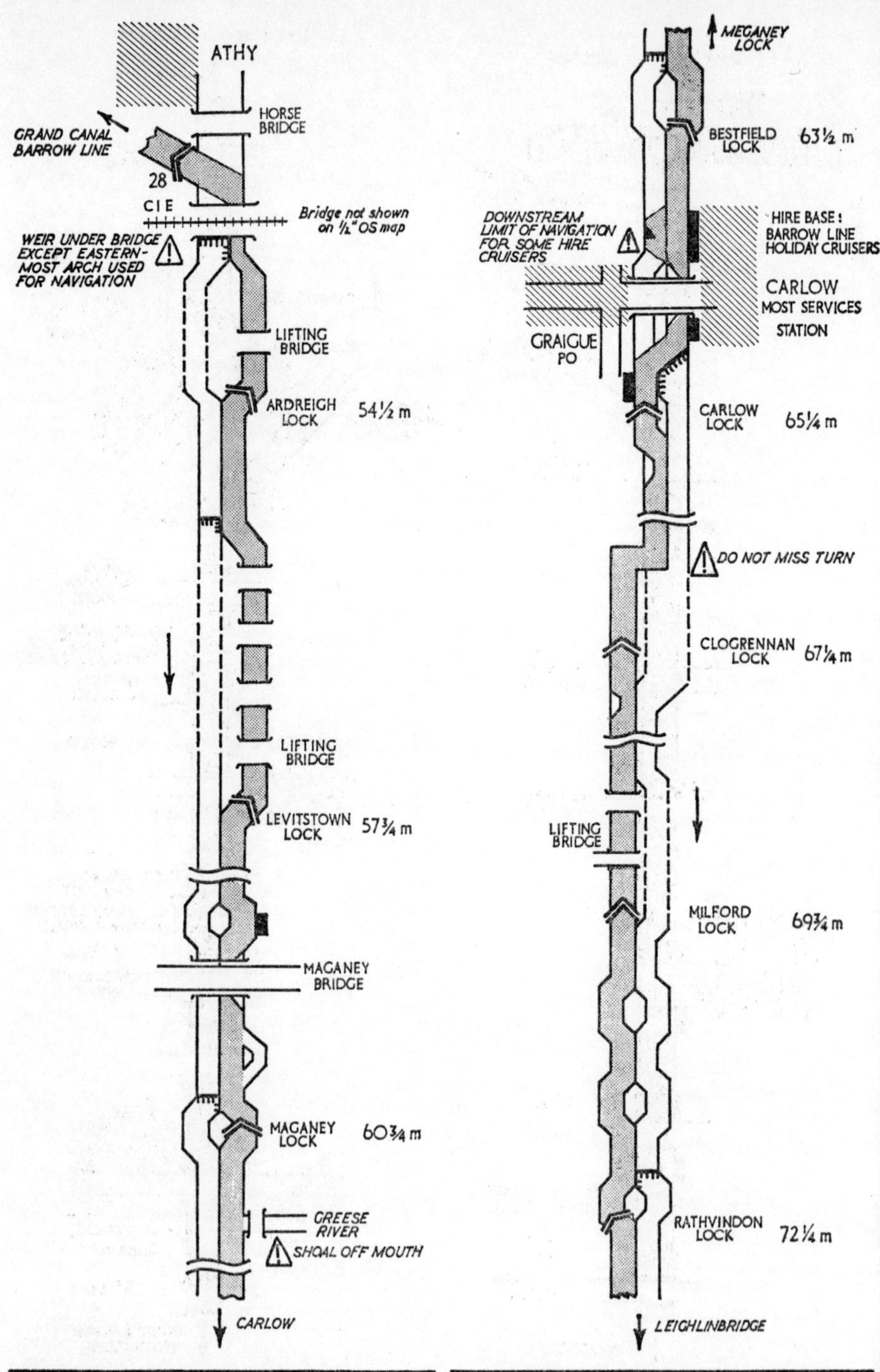

RIVER BARROW NAVIGATION 1

Distances in miles from First Lock, Grand Canal

See pp 83–4

RIVER BARROW NAVIGATION 2

Distances in miles from First Lock, Grand Canal

See pp 84, 87

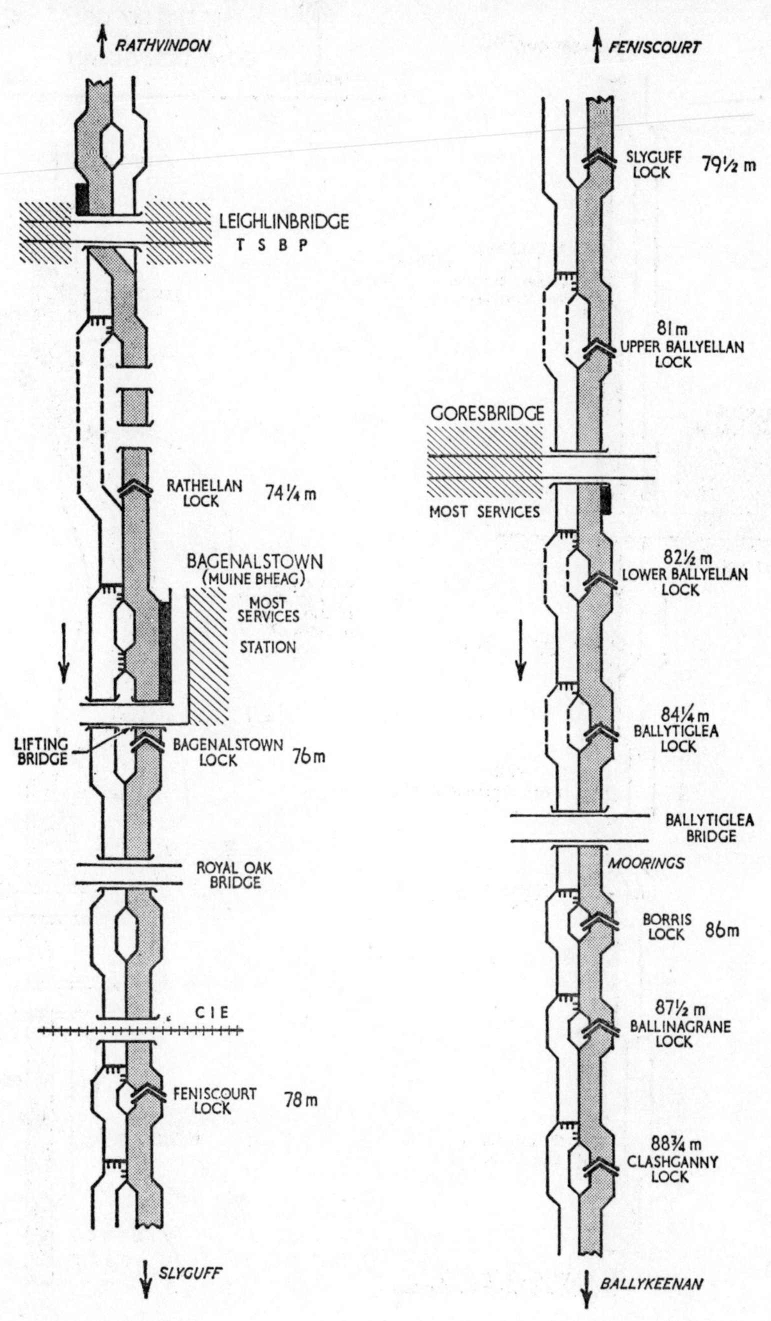

RIVER BARROW NAVIGATION 3

Distances in miles from First Lock, Grand Canal

See pp 87–8

RIVER BARROW NAVIGATION 4

Distances in miles from First Lock, Grand Canal

See pp 88–9

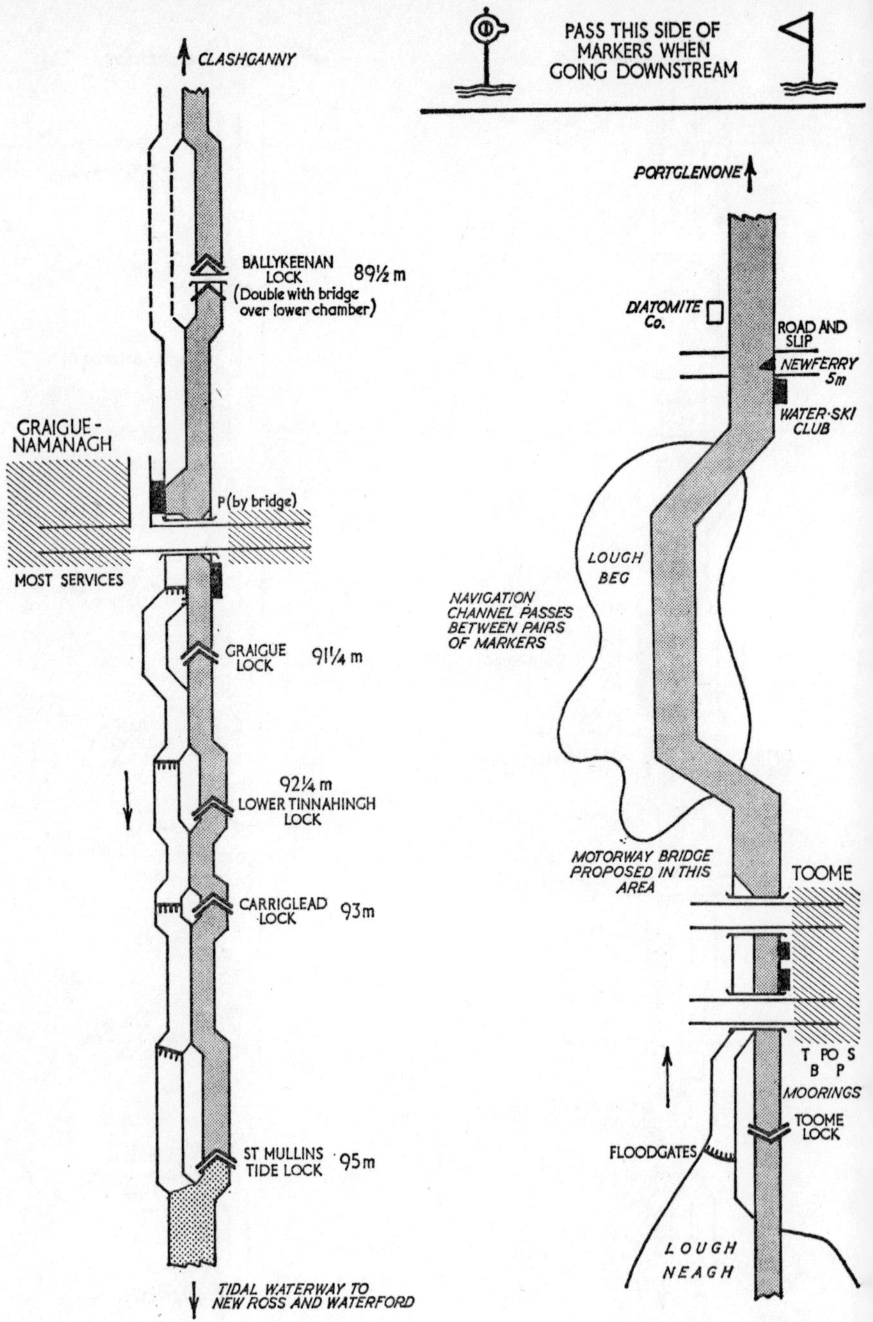

RIVER BARROW NAVIGATION 5

Distance in miles from First Lock, Grand Canal

See pp 89–90

LOWER BANN NAVIGATION 1

Approximate distances in miles from Toome lock

See pp 122–3

PASS THIS SIDE OF MARKERS

PASS THIS SIDE OF MARKERS

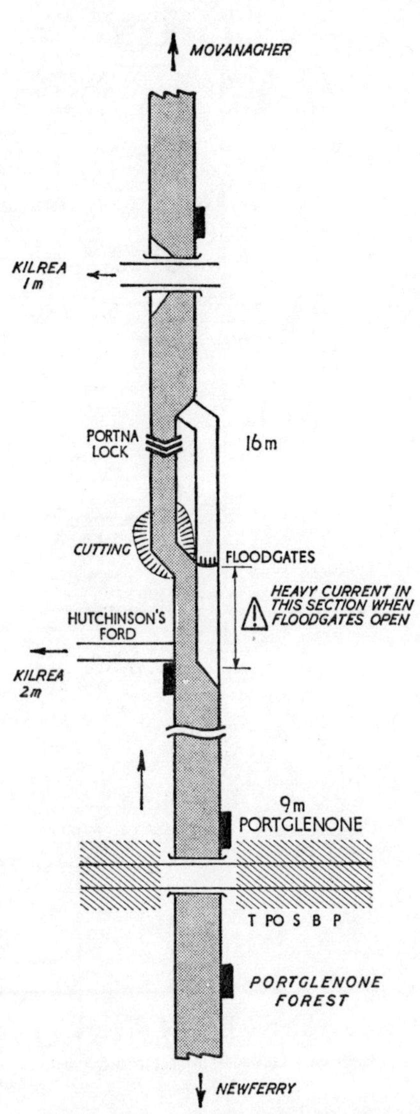

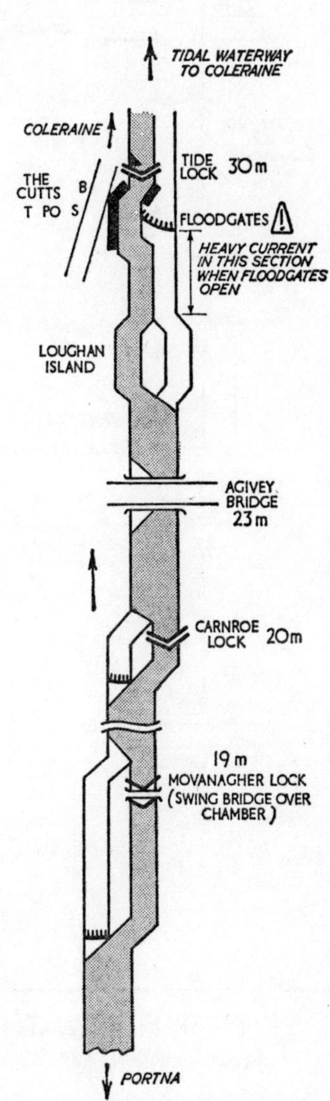

LOWER BANN NAVIGATION 2

Approximate distances in miles from Toome lock

See p 123

LOWER BANN NAVIGATION 3

Approximate distances in miles from Toome lock

See pp 123, 126

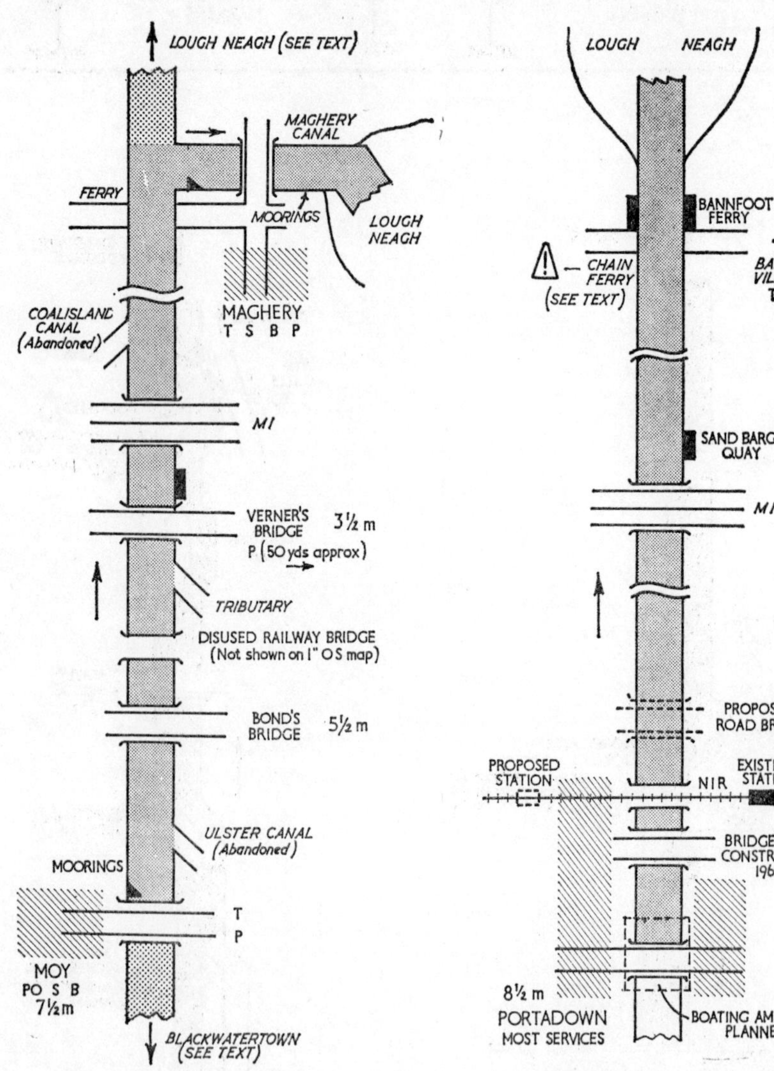

RIVER BLACKWATER

Approximate distances in miles from Maghery

See pp 127–8

UPPER BANN RIVER

Approximate distances in miles from Bannfoot Ferry

See pp 128–9

Useful Addresses

Addresses of hire operators are given in Chapter One and those of navigation and similar authorities in the appropriate chapter for each waterway. The following are also useful:

Charter Boat Association of Ireland,
18 Berkeley Street,
Dublin 7,
Irish Republic.

Erne Charter Boat Association:
Chairman (1969):
Ian C. Eadie,
The Limes,
Lisbellaw,
Co Fermanagh,
Northern Ireland.

Irish Hire Boat Operators Ltd (Penguin Group),
23 Clyde Road,
Dublin 4,
Irish Republic.

Inland Waterways Association of Ireland:
Hon Secretary (1970):
Sean Glennon,

6 Prospect Terrace,
Sandymount,
Dublin 4,
Irish Republic.

River Bann Association:
Hon Secretary (1969):
Dr D. Downing,
Lisconnan House,
Dervock,
Co Antrim,
Northern Ireland.

Bord Failte Eireann (Irish Tourist Board),
Baggot Street Bridge,
Dublin 2,
Irish Republic.

Northern Ireland Tourist Board,
10 Royal Avenue,
Belfast BT1 1DQ,
Northern Ireland.

Coras Iompair Eireann (Headquarters),
Heuston Station,
Dublin 8,
Irish Republic.

Northern Ireland Railways Co Ltd,
1 York Road,
Belfast BT15 1NG,
Northern Ireland.

Ulsterbus Ltd,
Milewater Road,
Belfast BT3 9BG,
Northern Ireland.

Bibliography

Green and Silver by L. T. C. Rolt remains the outstanding book on Irish waterways, although much has changed since the voyage it describes over the Grand and Royal Canals and the Shannon in 1948. For example, the Royal is now of interest to historians rather than navigators; and elsewhere the appearance of a 'yacht', in those fuel-scarce times a nine-days' wonder, is now commonplace, but the barges that were then familiar are now only a memory. *Green and Silver* and the works listed below have been consulted in writing this book, and those still obtainable make interesting further reading.

The Canals of the North of Ireland, W. A. McCutcheon, David & Charles.

Coastal Passenger Steamers and Inland Navigations in the North of Ireland, D. B. McNeill, Belfast Transport Museum.

Transport in Ireland 1880–1910, P. Flanagan, Transport Research Associates.

The Canals of the South of Ireland, V. T. H. and D. R. Delany, David & Charles.

Coastal Passenger Steamers and Inland Navigations in the South of Ireland, D. B. McNeill, Belfast Transport Museum.

Illustrated Ireland Guide, Bord Failte Eireann.

Facts about Ireland, Department of External Affairs, Dublin.

Northern Ireland—Its people, resources, history and government, H. Shearman, HMSO Belfast.

Voyage in a Bowler Hat, H. Malet, Hutchinson.
Where the River Shannon Flows, R. Hayward, Dundalgan Press.
The Shannon—River of loughs and legends, N. Nowlan, Frederick Muller.
Thanks for the Memory, H. J. Rice, Athlone Printing Works Co Ltd.
Pilot Book of the River Shannon, Bord Failte/IWAI.
The Shannon Guide, J. A. Dowling (Editor), Irish Shell & BP Ltd.
Waterways of the Republic of Ireland '68, G. Dibb (Editor), Link House Publications.
Irish Inland Waterways Holidays—Cruising on the Grand Canal, E. C. Barrett (Editor), Fodhla Printing Co.
Prospect of Erne, M. Rogers, Fermanagh Field Club.
Waterways of Northern Ireland '68, G. Dibb (Editor), Link House Publications.
Boating Guide to the River Bann and Lough Neagh, W. Clarke, Northern Ireland Tourist Board/River Bann Association.
Inland Waterways of Great Britain and Ireland, L. A. Edwards, Imray, Laurie, Norie, & Wilson Ltd.
Portrait of the Grand Canal, G. D'Arcy, Transport Research Associates.
In the Wake of the Gods, H. Malet, Chatto & Windus.
Annual Reports of the IWAI.

Acknowledgements

Many people have assisted me to prepare this book; I am most grateful to them, and particularly indebted to the following: Mrs R. Heard, Dr P. Denham, P. Dobbs; J. Carty, K. Sloane, M. Webb, A. Pocock, O'B. Kennedy, J. Weaving; J. Dalton, R. F. Shirley, J. H. Scott; M. Semple, the Dolan Bros of Galway; I. Eadie, R. Smyth, W. Thomas, V. Barham; J. McHenry, B. W. Musgrave, J. McGarry, Dr D. Downing, A. Smith; J. P. Murray, B. Hogan; D. McGimpsey, J. Crichton; many operators of hire craft and officials of the various waterways and the Electricity Supply Board, Bord na Mona, the Automobile Association, the Irish Embassy in London, HM Customs and Excise, and the Revenue Commissioners; and the friends who joined me on voyages of exploration and submitted to being hustled on to see if there was a petrol pump or a post office at the next bridge when it would have been so much pleasanter to have sat still in the sun to fish or sketch or just have another drink.

Index

Where several page numbers are shown against one entry, principal references in bold type should be consulted first.

Index

Index

Index